WELLSPRING

"Above all else,

guard your heart,

for it is the wellspring of life."

Proverbs 4:23

Other books by Stephen Macchia:

Becoming A Healthy Church

Becoming A Healthy Church Workbook

Becoming A Healthy Disciple

Becoming A Healthy Disciple: Small Group Study and Worship Guide

Becoming A Healthy Team

Becoming A Healthy Team Exercises

Beloved Disciple

Crafting A Rule of Life

WELLSPRING

*31 Days to
Whole-Hearted Living*

STEPHEN A. MACCHIA

LEADERSHIP
TRANSFORMATIONS INC.
FORMATION | DISCERNMENT | RENEWAL

Published by Leadership Transformations
P.O. Box 338, Lexington, MA 02420
www.leadershiptransformations.org

May 2014
Printed in the United States of America.

Library of Congress Cataloging-in-Publication Data
Macchia, Stephen A., 1956–
Wellspring: 31 Days to Whole-Hearted Living / Stephen A. Macchia.
Includes bibliographical references.
ISBN 978-0-692-22571-4 (pbk.)
Religion / Christian Life / Devotional

Dedicated to

Rueben P. Job

Spiritual Mentor, Encouraging Friend, and
Beloved Brother in Christ

Table of Contents

Introduction: With All My Heart

The Bible refers to at least 50 different terms describing the various conditions of our heart. Words such as broken and contrite, discerning, hardened, devoted, foolish, pure, wounded, and undivided. This book will be looking at these terms one entry at a time and will invite you to consider them for 31 days in a row and in light of your own heart condition during this season of your life with God.

The one word that jumps out the most from the biblical text is "all" my heart. There are dozens of places where we are urged to know, love, serve, obey, trust, desire, seek, and extol God with *all* of our heart. Not just a portion of our hearts, as if it can be partitioned into segments of halves, thirds, quarters, fifths or tenths. No, with *all* of our heart, as well as *all* of our soul, mind and strength… nothing held back for ourselves – *all* of our heart given *all* for God and for *all* the purposes and pleasure of God.

When we love God with all of our heart, we are coming to the conclusion that he in fact wants all of our heart. We are acknowledging our need for God to reign supreme in our heart. We are professing our desperate need for God to take over every dark, distant, disillusioned part of our hearts and heal us from the inside out. We are saying yes to his invitation to trust and obey so that with all of our heart we may discover more and more of his heart for us and for our world. With all our heart we love God and follow after His personal rule of life for us – declaring every part of our lives in submission to God's heart (see how others have inclined all their heart in God's direction at www.RuleOfLife.com).

Loving God with all our heart is an invitation worth affirming, celebrating, claiming and living. In fact, don't just make this choice for your own sake, impress it on your children, talk about it along the road of life, tie it like a string of remembrance on your finger, bind this priority on your forehead, write it on the doorframes of your house and on your gates (cf. Deut. 6: 4-9). Inclining the entirety of your heart in God's direction will reap fruit beyond measure, fruit that will last a lifetime and into all eternity.

"All to Jesus I surrender, all to him I freely give...I surrender all, I surrender all, all to thee, my blessed Savior, I surrender all." These words from that historic hymn are challenging, to say the least. Easier to sing them than to live them, that's for sure. But, a heart fully surrendered to the Lord is one that's willing to offer all one's heart to God – nothing held back for selfish gain or ulterior motive. Surrendering our hearts into the loving hand of God is so liberating, and with that freedom comes a life of joy and delight.

Giving over all of our heart to God is a choice of the will – openly release all of your heart and watch what happens from deep within. The joy that will emerge will be life transforming for you and all who cross your path. Then, as you invite others to do the same, the ripple effects on your personal relationships and spiritual community will be transformational for all.

Is there a portion of your heart that you're not turning over to God today? Let this be an encouragement to you as on behalf of the Triune God I too invite you to love the Father, Son, and Holy Spirit with all of your heart. You will be glad you returned your heart to the One who created it within you in the first place.

"I will praise you, O Lord, with all my heart; I will tell of all your wonders. I will be glad and rejoice in you; I will sing praise to your name, O Most High" (Psalm 9:1).

"We are half-hearted creatures, fooling about with drink and sex and ambition when infinite joy is offered us, like an ignorant child who wants to go on making mud pies in a slum because he cannot imagine what is meant by the offer of a holiday at the sea. We are far too easily pleased."

-- C.S. Lewis

Day 1

The Hardened Heart

When the 21 year old Zedekiah became king of Judah (subsequently reigning in Jerusalem for eleven years), he did evil in the eyes of the Lord his God and did not humble himself before God or King Nebuchadnezzar. "He became stiff-necked and hardened his heart and would not turn to the Lord, the God of Israel" (2 Chronicles 36: 13). One of a string of kings who continually defied and defiled the ways of God and took matters into their own hands, Zedekiah mocked God's messengers and stood up against anything that would breathe godliness into his heart.

When we stand up against God's Word, defy His reign in our hearts and lives, we may not be as dramatic as Zedekiah but in fact our necks stiffen and our hearts harden nonetheless. Ever see such a display of arrogant exile of the heart? Ever experience it yourself? I recently confronted one such leader about the defiance in his heart toward God and those he was called to lead and serve. I could almost see his neck stiffen as he was confronted by the truth about God and himself. He didn't like what he was hearing and even though I could see a seared conscience, he resisted the invitation of God to soften his hardened heart. A sad sight indeed.

"Furthermore, all the leaders of the priests and the people became more and more unfaithful, following the detestable practices of the nations and defiling the temple of the Lord" (2 Chronicles 36: 14). The fruit of a hardened heart, and the sad reality, is unfaithfulness and defilement among others. The ripple effect of a stiff-necked person is that they espouse and encourage similar hearts to grow in others.

A hardened heart doesn't come overnight. It takes time to calcify a heart to the place where it becomes impenetrably rock hard. Some of the reasons why a heart is hardened include: deep hurt and heartache from one's past; pain that goes unattended or unhealed; cynicism that starts with brittleness toward the successes of others; critical spirits that go unchecked; bitterness toward those who are smarter, prettier, stronger, or wealthier; medical conditions that curtail what was a previously preferred normal. These and many other justifiable concerns that weigh heavy on one's heart can in fact harden a heart.

And the fruit of a hardened heart isn't much prettier than the reasons noted above. A hardened heart can be offensive to others; it can blind you to the goodness of others; it can bleed out on those who love and care for you deeply. In essence, a hard heart is impermeable, difficult to tolerate, and harsh in treatment toward the graciously naïve or innocent who surround you. Simply put, a hard heart is closed, opposed, self-protected, judgmental, and rigidly harsh.

The invitation from God is quite the contrary..."Today, if you hear his voice, do not harden your hearts" (Psalm 95: 7,8). Instead, let it be softened by God's Word, in prayer as you hear his still small voice, and in community as you are challenged to embrace the truth about God and oneself (which will set you free!) from a brother or sister who cares enough to confront a hardened heart. The world needs Christ-followers who confess their hardened heart and allow the Spirit to soften it for God's glory.

Will you be counted among those who are willing to have their hardened hearts softened by the fresh movement of God's Spirit within? If so, then working toward removing the callousness of your heart will be well worth the effort. Stay supple, pliable, and passionate about God and then watch how the Spirit rubs off the sharper edges of your hardened heart and forms you more and more into his likeness and for his glory.

Reflections on My Hardened Heart

_____
_____
_____
_____
_____
_____
_____
_____
_____
_____
_____
_____
_____
_____
_____
_____
_____
_____
_____
_____

Day 2

The Humble Heart

"Come to me, all you who are weary and burdened, and I will give you rest. Take my yoke upon you and learn from me, for I am gentle and humble in heart, and you will find rest for your souls. For my yoke is easy and my burden is light" (Matthew 11, 29, 30). Jesus is the perfect embodiment of a humble heart. He displays such a heart toward all who cross his path. He willingly humbles himself and gives up his life, even on the cross, for the sake of his followers. He humbly receives all responses to his life and ministry and doesn't fight back or stiff-arm anyone. His humility is contagious and beautiful. He invites us to humble our hearts and be filled up with God. Then and only then will we truly find rest for our souls.

As Jesus lovers and followers, we are to exhibit a humble heart – first and foremost toward God and then toward all who we know and serve. But, a humble heart begins with the choice of the will. "Humble yourself before the Lord" (James 4:10) as it emerges from the gift of God, for "God opposes the proud but gives grace to the humble" (James 4:6). These same two phrases are repeated in 1 Peter 5: 5,6 and wrapped up by verse 7, "Cast all your anxiety on him because he cares for you" which harkens back to Jesus' words previously quoted above.

A humble heart is evidence of a contrite heart. When we are willing to admit our brokenness and our desperate need for God, we humble ourselves before God and invite him to reign supremely in our hearts. When God's Spirit resides in the deepest crevices of our hearts and transforms us from the inside out, we are changed people. From such a humble heart we are available to love and serve others in Jesus' name. But, it begins with our desire to submit ourselves to God.

From a genuine act of submission, we enter into a vital union with God. No longer are we to be known exclusively by our name, but instead be identified with his Name. The Triune God – Father, Son, and Holy Spirit – is formed in unity and lived out in humble oneness. Humility begins and ends with and in God. This "perichoresis" of love is the perfect dance of the Trinity. As we enter the dance as children and heirs of the kingdom, as beloved brides of the Bridegroom himself, we are invited to embrace a life of humility. This humility grows outward from the heart.

Humility of heart is the opposite of pride and superiority. There simply isn't room in the body of Christ for that which is in opposition to the very heart and nature of God. Brokenness precedes humility, for the one who embraces humility is the one who fears God, loves God, worships God, and is known lovingly and intimately by God the Savior.

Jesus is the greatest and one and only perfected form of humanity, and the One who embodied humble hearted love. He always protected his alone time with the Father, but when he reemerged into and among the crowds he loved and served and witnessed out of humility. His life of grace, mercy, and peace modeled for his disciples the true meaning of the word humble. As such, Jesus was able to seamlessly invite his followers to do likewise. He came not to be served, but to serve, and to give his life as a humble ransom for many.

We learn true humility when we are willing to be like soil...dirt...humus...willing to be walked upon and mixed within the fertilizer of life. Humble souls are more aware of the needs of others than they are of themselves. Humus-like hearts are willing to look to Jesus as their example of humility and follow Jesus into places where he invites them to serve in his name. Resting in God, finding their hope in God, a humble heart discovers true rest for their souls. Are you willing to pursue a life that "acts justly, loves mercy, and walks humbly with God" (Micah 6: 8)? How is your pride to be broken, and replaced instead with humility today?

Day 2 Journal

Reflections on My Humble Heart

_____
_____
_____
_____
_____
_____
_____
_____
_____
_____
_____
_____
_____
_____
_____
_____
_____
_____
_____
_____
_____
_____

Day 3

The Deceitful Heart

"The heart is deceitful above all things and beyond cure. Who can understand it?" says the prophet Jeremiah (Jer. 17: 9). He previously judges similar hearts, "Friend deceives friend, and no one speaks the truth. They have taught their tongues to lie; they weary themselves with sinning" (Jeremiah 9: 5). So beware of the deceiver and the slanderer and all who speak not the truth.

Our mouths speak forth that which is in the heart. If truth is in the heart, truths will be spoken. If lies are in the heart, lies will be spoken. Sometimes the lies we have believed are about a god we think we understand. But, it's a false god when what we believe about God isn't based on the truth of his Word. Many think they know God but when their mouths give voice to that knowledge it can sound more like shame, ridicule, condemnation, judgment, or constant rebuke. Sadly, many lie about their god and many others believe their words.. That's not the God we know as loving Father, forgiving Son, and empowering Spirit.

We can also lie about ourselves and others. We say things about ourselves that are untruths...and we are self- deceived. We say false things about others...and we deceive many more. Deception is beguilement, bluff, mystification, bad faith, and subterfuge, all acts to propagate beliefs that are not true, or not the whole truth (as in half-truths or omission). Deception can involve dissimulation, propaganda, and sleight of hand. It can employ distraction, camouflage or concealment. All of which when employed toward a friend or family member wreaks havoc on relationships.

When others lie about themselves or about you, they destroy friendship and community. Lies and deceit can cut deeply into the fabric of relationships, sometimes beyond the ability to mend. A deceitful heart isn't created overnight. To embellish one story is sad enough, but to develop a habit of lie-telling grows deeply rooted thorns that choke the heart and destroy the lives of all who reside close to such weeds. So many today, even in the body of Christ, are used to living deceitfully that it often takes a dramatic wake up call to bring one back to the truth.

I have seen the destruction and dismantling of relationships first hand when deceitful hearts have the upper hand. It's demoralizing and debilitating for all involved. When such deceit is in ones heart toward God, it leads to eternal damnation. When deceit is in the center of human relationships, there is a separation that often goes unresolved. The antidote to deceit is truth. Knowing truth, living truth, and speaking truth will indeed set people free to fully live and fully receive the love that comes from the God of Truth to set free their captivity of deception.

What lies have others spoken of you (you're no good; you're stupid; you're ugly) or you believed about yourself (I'm no good; I'm stupid; I'm ugly) that would be life changing if released and revealed as truth? What lies have you heard from the lips of another that need to be exposed and turned upside down by truth (are you willing to be bold enough to lovingly confront the lie and/or the liar)? What lies have you given voice to that need to be confessed and forgiven, by God and by others in your sphere of influence? With boldness and courage of heart, may you become an ambassador for truth and a dispenser of grace toward all who walk in the darkness of deceit and need to be liberated by the truth that will set them free.

"Heal me, O Lord, and I will be healed; save me and I will be saved, for you are the one I praise" (Jeremiah 17: 14). Be free to love and serve with truth in your heart and love on your lips!

Day 3 Journal

Reflections on
My Deceitful Heart

_____

_____

_____

_____

_____

_____

_____

_____

_____

_____

_____

_____

_____

_____

_____

_____

_____

_____

Day 4

Day 4

∽

The Grateful Heart

In the Apostle Paul's "Rule of Life" for the Colossians, he urges them to "Let the peace of Christ rule in your hearts, since as members of one body you were called to peace. And be thankful. Let the Word of Christ dwell in you richly as you teach and admonish one another with all wisdom, and as you sing psalms, hymns and spiritual songs with gratitude in your hearts to God. And whatever you do, whether in word or deed, do it all in the name of the Lord Jesus, giving thanks to God the Father through him" (Colossians 3: 15-17). Notice his emphases at the end of each encouragement: be thankful, with gratitude, giving thanks.

A grateful heart is a blessed and joyful heart. Gratitude is the source of both. When we are grateful for our salvation, grateful for the grace extended to us so generously from God, grateful for the gift of life, every breath we are privileged to breathe, then our hearts are overflowing with love. A grateful heart is in essence a loving heart. Who among us doesn't like to hear the words "thank you" or "I'm grateful to God for you" or "how grateful I am for life: whether in suffering, in plenty, or in want." Yes, a grateful heart is a gift to the one who's thankful and to all who cross their path.

When you examine your life, even the past 24 hours, for what or whom are you most grateful? This entry is being written just three days after Ruth's and my wedding anniversary. I am profoundly grateful to the Lord for the gift of my precious wife. I am giving voice to my gratitude to both God and directly to her so that the giver of the gift and the gift herself can know of my heart's true delight. I treasure the gift of Ruth and when she knows of my grateful heart I can see her heart swell; when I deny her of my gratitude I can see her heart shrivel. O Lord, may you continue to ripen within me a grateful heart!

A grateful heart finds reasons to be thankful even when the outward expression of life feels hopelessly dark and dreary. When our hearts are imprisoned by the circumstances around us that leave us discouraged, disillusioned, or disheartened, it's hard to even whisper a word of thanks. But, the biblical text and the lives of faithful men and women in the history of the Church remind us to give thanks no matter what comes our way. That's why the apostle Paul reminds the church in Colossae to be grateful. They were living in hard times; life wasn't easy; the Christian life was filled with sacrifice and hardship. And yet the invitation was to be grateful.

Can you find reasons to be grateful today, for all that's delightful about your life, as well as the hardships you and others around you are encountering today? For some redemptive meaning and purpose, God is allowing you to experience the suffering and heartache that's a part of your life today. In response to what he is permitting, can you even offer a whisper of thanksgiving? When we can open up our hearts to receive all of life – the good, the bad, and the ugly – then a response of gratitude is possible.

But, when we close up our hearts and rebelliously refuse to receive the harder, challenging, and more painful parts of life, then thanksgiving is left on the doorstep and out in the cold parched air of ingratitude.

Gratitude begins with the awareness of all that God has given to us thus far in life. When we have a grateful heart we are led into a deeper fellowship with the God of grace, goodness, and generosity. Each time I hear a story of how God has so sweetly developed gratitude in the heart of his followers, my heart grows with thankfulness and joy. Listen for yourself to the testimonies of others around you who freely share their thankfulness to you - and allow your heart to blossom with renewed gratitude. May others know you as a grateful person as you continually express thanks for the myriad of gifts you've been entrusted with in this abundant life.

Day 4

Journal: Reflections on My Grateful Heart

_____

_____

_____

_____

_____

_____

_____

_____

_____

_____

_____

_____

_____

_____

_____

_____

_____

_____

_____

_____

_____

Day 5

❧

The Foolish Heart

"The fool says in his heart 'There is no God'" Psalm 14:1. To deny God is to foster a foolish heart. Period. End of thought.

But, there are many other manifestations of foolishness of heart toward others, and the Proverbs are filled with insight here. "A chattering fool comes to ruin" (10:10) and "Whoever spreads slander is a fool" (10:18) and "A fool shows his annoyance" (12:16) and "A fool is hotheaded and reckless" (14:16) and "A fool spurns his father's discipline" (15:5) and "Every fool is quick to quarrel" (20:3) and "A fool repeats his folly" (26:11) and "A fool gives full vent to his anger" (29:11).

Foolishness comes in all sorts of shapes and sizes. Fools consider their heart as their own and left to their own devices end up foolishly inconsiderate toward all others. It's almost as if a foolish heart is the ancient term for what we know today as a narcissist. A self-absorbed person is unable to see anyone else but themselves. Therefore, to act in such unbecoming ways isn't seen by the narcissist. There is no clear self-awareness to a fool. Others can see it in them, experience their world by projection, and suffer (often quietly) as a result.

Another word for a fool is clown. Someone who adorns him/herself with a mask that is painted on with great care, so that anything of deeper sensibilities may never be seen. A clown lives on the surface of life, always needing a fix of fun to keep away any form of reality. A clown wears a costume that's adorned with loud colors, bright labels, oversized shoes, large features, unkempt hair, expanded features, and ridiculous clothing to mask what's underneath and masquerade around all aspects of life. A clown is funny for a time, but foolish when seen over and over and over again.

Yet another image of a fool is one who has recklessly abandoned the strong foundation offered and has chosen instead a life of immoral, impure, or illegal behavior. This is the fool who knows better and selects instead a life that leads to destruction of self and others. Often this fool has been ridiculed or reduced to this behavior due to life circumstances beyond one's control, and in that case we empathize and prayerfully and compassionately reach out to save. For others, there is a choice of the will so strongly pronounced that bucks the system or radicalizes the establishment to the place where there is little one can do to help rectify beyond praying and waiting for this fool to come to his senses and turn back home once more. Either way, such fools are sad to see.

When have you seen a foolish heart lately? And, in what ways has your own heart led you down foolish paths yourself? When "fools" submit to God, He imparts them with wisdom. That's the grand irony of the gospel. God takes the foolishness of the cross and transforms it into the outstretched arms of love. God takes the foolish heart and makes it wise, courageous, eternally focused. "For the foolishness of God is wiser than man's wisdom, and the weakness of God is stronger than man's strength" (1 Cor. 1:26). I love the upside down nature of God and His Gospel unto our Salvation!

So, my friend, stop looking over your shoulder at the foolish heart of another and look inwardly and prayerfully toward your own foolishness of heart. Allow the Spirit to renew your heart and revive it into a wise and discerning heart. Invite God to lavish his forgiving love upon the foolish places in your heart where you have denied him full access. Then watch how God himself takes that which was previously foolish and makes it all brand new. That's the power and the glory of the Gospel of Jesus Christ and to him alone belongs all dominion, honor, and praise.

Day 5

Journal: Reflections on My Foolish Heart

_____

_____

_____

_____

_____

_____

_____

_____

_____

_____

_____

_____

_____

_____

_____

_____

_____

_____

_____

Day 6

∽

The Undivided Heart

The psalmist David writes such magnificent prayers! In Psalm 86, notice how the heart of David cries out for more of the Lord…

"Hear, O Lord, and answer me, for I am poor and needy…Guard my life, for I am devoted to you…Have mercy on me, O Lord, for I call to you all day long. Bring joy to your servant, for to you, O Lord, I lift up my soul…You are kind and forgiving, abounding in love to all who call to you…You are great and do marvelous deeds; you alone are God. Teach me your way, O Lord, and I will walk in your truth; give me

an undivided heart, that I may fear your name."
(Psalm 86: 1-6; 10,11)

David acknowledges that the Lord is great
in love, the one who delivered his soul. He's
compassionate, gracious, slow to anger, abounding
in love and faithfulness. In return, the psalmist
longs for a heart that's undivided. An undivided
heart is so filled up with God that there's no room
for any evil intent, arrogance, malice, vice or
pride. An undivided heart instead seeks purity of
thought, intimacy of fellowship, loving worship,
and unity of life purpose with God.

When the Lord gave the land back to the
Israelites, as he had promised, the prophet Ezekiel
records for us that the Lord "Will give them an
undivided heart and put a new spirit in them; I
will remove from them their heart of stone and
give them a heart of flesh. Then they will follow
my decrees and be careful to keep my laws.
They will be my people, and I will be their God."
(Ezekiel 11: 18-21). From a heart like impenetrable
stone to one likened to malleable flesh – what a
gift of transforming mercy and grace.

The competition for the heart of a believer is likened to warfare. An undivided heart knows how real the battle is within, as the enemy prowls around the heart seeking full control. The enemy tempts us with alluring pleasures, earthly pursuits, and worldly possessions. An undivided heart leans fully on the strength and power of the Holy Spirit to confront the enemy's schemes. That which divides the heart today keeps one from experiencing the fullness of the God-abundant life of Christlikeness. We cannot serve two masters.

For some, the heart is divided between extremes. On one hand, the heart is one of love, compassion, and joy. On the other hand, the heart can be filled with hatred, enmity and malice. To be so divided is the reality of a human heart that's drenched with both grace and guile. Such hearts – our hearts – need to be cleansed and forgiven, restored and renewed on a daily basis. For our hearts to go from divided to undivided, we need the work of God's Spirit to align our divided hearts with his loving and graciously undivided heart.

For still others, the heart can be divided between good and best, or between one option and an equally safe alternative. We can choose to pursue a cause that's meaningful, and then feel torn when another worthwhile entity comes our way. When choices and options are before us, and both seem acceptable, then prayerful discernment is needed to aid the process in order to leave one behind while embracing the other. Many strive in this regard and are successful in releasing one option for another, while others still dream about what was left behind and have trouble letting go, detaching from one in order to fully attach to the other.

So, what is it that's dividing your heart today and pulling you away from living fully for the Lord? Acknowledge the reality of your heart today and put your hope, confidence, and trust in God's lovingly faithful and forgiving hands. Put words or phrases together that describe what's keeping your heart divided, and entrust them prayerfully into the loving hands of God to lead you toward an undivided heart.

Day 6

Journal: Reflections on My Undivided Heart

Day 7

❦

The Adulterous Heart

In the Sermon on the Mount, Jesus said to the crowds, "You have heard that it was said, 'Do not commit adultery.' But I tell you that anyone who looks at a woman lustfully has already committed adultery with her in his heart." (Matthew 5: 27, 28) Here Jesus is quoting from Exodus 20: 14, the 7th of The 10 Commandments, with an emphasis on looking lustfully with the eyes as he defines the essence or core of an adulterous heart.

Then, Jesus continues with the harsh analogy of gouging out your right eye if it causes you to sin, for it would be better to lose one part of the body than to have your whole person thrown into hell. In other words, he challenges his hearers to consider the ramifications of one bad choice (looking lustfully), which can lead to much larger consequences (an adulterous heart) and eventual acts of infidelity.

Today the heart is greatly tempted by viewing pornography, the place where lust is most dramatically exploited, encouraged, and embodied for this generation. The pornography industry in America today is estimated to exceed $10 billion/year, and is larger than the NFL, NBA, and Major League Baseball combined. With an estimated 420 million pages of pornography available online, 13,000 new porn videos released annually, and 900 million videos available for sale or rent, one can't help but be concerned about how this is shaping our gender and sexual identities, as well as our relationships.

Amazingly, the pornography industry is legal and oft-promoted as socially acceptable, as it has become a part of today's cultural and economic mainstream. But, it is destroying hearts, homes, and relationships 24/7 all around the globe. Now considered one of the fastest growing addictions among young, impressionable adolescent males, as well as a large percentage of men (especially those under the age of 30 who grew up with ease of accessibility to the internet), looking lustfully has become a way of life. Media of almost every type make lust of the heart ripe for the picking.

But, the lustful look and the adulterous heart isn't simply a man's issue or problem. Women also struggle with their own lustful temptations (and many accompany their male counterparts in the world of pornography). Adultery has no distinct gender or age boundaries, or other lines of demarcation. The need for purity of heart exists for all. So, how will you pray for those who wrestle with sexual temptation? How will you come alongside them with compassionate empathy and support? And, most importantly, how will you maintain your own purity of heart?

Jesus' words ring true today, and it should break our hearts and realign our prayers for all who struggle with and ultimately succumb to this temptation. And this temptation is in all of us, if we're truly honest. There lurks within us an interest in tapping into our lust for life, most boldly evident in our sexual desires. That's why the apostle Paul includes "self control" as an evidence of or fruit of the Spirit. Self-control is the issue. But not self-control that comes from our own inner strength, but instead one that evolves from a life lived in the Spirit. Only the Spirit of God can help you (and me) conquer our lustful thoughts and actions. Only the Spirit can give us the strength to look the other way, consider inner beauty more important than outward adornment, and/or say no to our overpowering temptations.

Previous to his statements about the adulterous heart, Jesus also said, "Blessed are the pure in heart, for they will see God" (Matthew 5: 8). May the eyes of our hearts search earnestly for God and focus our attention on all that honors and pleases him. May it be so for your heart even today.

Day 7

Journal: Reflections on My Adulterous Heart

_____

_____

_____

_____

_____

_____

_____

_____

_____

_____

_____

_____

_____

_____

_____

_____

_____

_____

_____

_____

_____

Day 8

⁂

The Gentle Heart

I recently had the unique opportunity to meet one of my living heroes for the very first time. His name is Rueben Job, an 87 year old retired Methodist Bishop. He's the author and compiler of several books that have dramatically impacted my personal spiritual life, especially his Guide to Prayer series published by Upper Room. We use his materials extensively at Leadership Transformations, on our retreats, among our board/team/donor family, and with seminary students at Gordon-Conwell. I was deeply touched by this encounter with a man after God's heart, who embodies one word: gentleness. I've since had the privilege of being with Rueben several times since that first encounter – what a gift.

Having never met my colleague, Rick Anderson, or myself, Rueben and his wife Beverly welcomed us with open arms into their home in a lovely retirement community just outside Nashville, Tennessee. Rueben has been following with interest the development of LTI since our inception in July 2003, has offered words of encouragement to our ministry family, and recently wrote an endorsement for my book *Crafting A Rule of Life* (www.RuleOfLife.com/ endorsements/) He sat with us in his living room, shared openly about his life story and his love for God's Word, the Church, and his family. He opened several windows into his own soul, and paid close attention to the state of our souls as well. It was an encounter drenched with the sweet, gentle aroma of Christ.

Rueben reminded me of my own grandfather, another gentle man of God. These men remind me that the word gentleness is very close to the word gentleman. Who do you know who truly embodies that word? Jesus was gentle and humble of heart (Matt. 11:29) and he encouraged gentleness among his disciples and followers. The Apostle Paul spoke often of gentleness too:

be completely humble and gentle (Eph. 4:2); let your gentleness be evident to all (Phil. 4:5); clothe yourselves with compassion, kindness, humility, gentleness and patience (Col. 3:12); and includes gentleness as a fruit of the Spirit (Gal. 5:23).

As I reflect on meeting Rueben Job, consider prayerfully the biblical definition of gentleness, and then turn on the television to listen to political pundits and candidates, movie stars and business leaders, society's super heroes and all who occupy air time, I'm startled by which kind of life and message is most endearing. A gentle heart expresses gentle words, thoughts, attitudes, and actions. A gentle heart is what most comforts the downtrodden and heals brokenness. A gentle heart is sensitive to God and the needs of others. A gentle heart is not puffed up with pride, instead considers others more important than self. A gentle heart evokes a similar response.

It's fair to say that not only did Rueben express gentleness, but his wife Beverly did too. Beverly is dripping with gentleness from the time you meet her until the moment you say farewell. Her smile, demeanor, and interest in your story is a shining example as well to what it means to be gentle of heart. She welcomed us with open arms, practiced hospitality like few others, and we left her presence better men as a result.

I share the story of the Job's in hopes that their example will spark a memory or relationship that helps you recall the beauty of gentleness. In what ways are you most drawn to gentleness? In what ways might God be calling you to abide in a spirit of gentleness toward all who cross your path today, even toward those who are the most difficult for you to love? Pursue faith, love, endurance and gentleness, and then invite God to blossom from within you a gentleness of heart.

Day 8

Journal: Reflections on My Gentle Heart

_____

_____

_____

_____

_____

_____

_____

_____

_____

_____

_____

_____

_____

_____

_____

_____

_____

_____

_____

Day 9

❧

The Stubborn Heart

When the preacher on Sunday morning mentioned the sinfulness of stubbornness, my conscience was pricked and my attentiveness was raised. Where is there a latent or obvious form of stubbornness within my heart? What about for you; is there stubbornness within you that keeps you from living the abundant Christian life?

Stubbornness is a nasty attribute. Some variant of the word stubborn appears 28 times in the Bible, and it's also referred an additional 19 times as "stiff-necked." Regardless of the exact term, God is deeply distressed by stubborn hearts. He delights when we let go of our stubbornness and return to him.

When God's people follow "the stubbornness of their evil hearts" (Jeremiah 11:8), they show forth how "the heart is deceitful above all things and beyond cure" (Jeremiah 17:9) without the Lord. When we follow the "stubborn inclinations of our evil hearts" it only leads us "backward and not forward" (Jeremiah 7:24). Left to our own self-absorbed choices, God at times gives us "over to our stubborn hearts to follow our own desires" (Psalm 81: 11,12).

Stubbornness is expressed in a myriad of ways. Sometimes stubbornness is obvious...hearing the word no to every request no matter how large or small; being locked in verbal combat when certain issues are raised that one rarely or never sees differently; refusal to do or say something that would build up another; even making choices and living out convictions that are good but will never change, can be an expression of stubbornness as well. Those with the propensity to show forth their stubbornness, often without any self-awareness, are the easiest ones to tag with the label of stubborn.

At other times, stubbornness is not so readily apparent. Persons who are equally as stubborn as those who show it outwardly can indeed be stubborn, and yet are more cautious or even silent in their ways of relating. Some express their stubbornness in passive aggressive ways, taking control of the situation through strictness of will but absence of expression. Others might simply not respond at all and stubbornly refuse to engage mentally, socially, spiritually, or physically. They may feel threatened and simply back off from any meaningful participation, but stubborn nonetheless.

Responding in submission to the Lord is the only spiritual antidote to stubbornness. Returning to God prayerfully and choosing to obey him as Lord and King of our hearts is the only way to meaningfully reverse a stubborn heart. Because of God's gracious and merciful love for his children, he stands on the porch of heaven waiting patiently for us to come to our senses and turn our hearts toward home. When we do so, his loving embrace leads us back into a life of strength that grows out of a renewed longing for sweet surrender.

What about our stubbornness toward one another as members of the family of God? Those who have an overpowering need to be right all the time leave no room for another opinion and no room for joy in the relationship. It's hard to work with a stubborn person. It's difficult to be married to a stubborn person. Stubborn people always have to get their way, often at the expense of their relationships. They have no clue about the values of flexibility, listening, and a teachable spirit.

Is it time to end your dogged determination of hanging on obstinately to a dead end proposition, attitude, right, or opinion? Instead, humble yourself and pray that God in his infinite love and mercy will lead you to a heart that's renewed from the inside out. Then, seek out those you may have hurt by your stubborn heart and be reconciled. There's freedom on the opposite side of stubbornness. What's your choice today?

Day 9

Journal: Reflections on My Stubborn Heart

_____

_____

_____

_____

_____

_____

_____

_____

_____

_____

_____

_____

_____

_____

_____

_____

_____

_____

_____

Day 10

∝

The Discerning Heart

I'm composing this entry in the midst of helping our daughter Rebekah move to Denver, Colorado. She's been in a process of transition for the past ten months, beginning with a desire to join her best friend who's there as a seminary student studying spiritual formation and soul care. The final decision to move came several months ago, and included lots of thoughtful discussions, personal deliberations, and financial considerations. Now her dream has become a reality and we're delighted with the prayerful discernment process she has undertaken in the context of her community of family and friends.

Discernment is a matter of the heart. It begins and ends with a sense of God's Spirit moving in, through, and among those engaged in the process. Discernment involves an awareness of God's presence and power, and often includes decision-making both great and small. Some have the gift of discernment (a subject for another time), but all Christ followers are invited to engage in discernment throughout their faith journey.

One of the clearest biblical stories of discernment is found in Luke 24, and the scene is the Road to Emmaus (verses 13-35). During this encounter with the risen Christ, two of his disciples were forlorn and confused about the death of their beloved Jesus. When Jesus shows up and walks along with them, he answers their questions and speaks into their experience. The whole encounter is drenched with Scriptural wisdom, compassionate insight and empathetic love. "When he was at the table with them, he took bread, gave thanks, broke it and began to give it to them. Then their eyes were opened and they recognized him...they asked each other, 'Were not our hearts burning within us while he talked with us on the road and opened the

Scriptures to us?'" What a great discernment question!

Discernment occurs all along the journey of life when our hearts are burning within us, due to the empowering awareness of the Spirit. Sometimes God's presence and power is obvious to his disciples and movement toward Jesus and his will is smooth and seamless. At other times there seems to be no sense of his guiding hand and we need to simply pray and wait for direction. Still other decisions require a process that leads toward clarity and consolation prior to moving forward. All of these incidences are faith producing and guide us into a deeper more intimate walk with the Savior.

Consider the ways in which discernment is currently a part of your Christian life: in your decisions to be made, relationships to be deepened, future directions to be determined by your family or team. Precedent to the discernment of choices is the discerning of God's presence. Like the disciples on the Road to Emmaus, we too need to pause and reflect and notice God right there by our side, making himself known to us in his Word, in prayer, in the beauty of creation, and in the love of spiritual community. The more we are aware of his presence, the more we will look to him for love and guidance all along the journey we know as life.

Where in your faith walk is God inviting you into a time of prayerful discernment? Check out www.RuleOfLife.com and see how others are leaning into this experience with joyful anticipation. I echo with gladness for you the prayer of the Apostle Paul for his friends in Philippi, "That your love may abound more and more in knowledge and depth of insight, so that you may be able to discern what is best and may be pure and blameless until the day of Christ, filled with the fruit of righteousness that comes through Jesus Christ – to the glory and praise of God" (Phil. 1: 9-11).

Day 10

Journal: Reflections on My Discerning Heart

_____

_____

_____

_____

_____

_____

_____

_____

_____

_____

_____

_____

_____

_____

_____

_____

_____

_____

_____

_____

_____

Day 11

❦

The Jealous Heart

While my wife and I were taking a leisurely afternoon stroll in a quaint community near our home, I overheard a few conversations standing in line at a coffee shop and sitting outside on a park bench. The first was about the couple's second home on Cape Cod. The second was in reference to the luxury vehicle one man had just purchased for his daughter. What was it about their casual comments that tugged on me? I don't like to admit it, but both sparked a tinge of jealousy in my heart…a response I neither desired nor appreciated. I was surprised how quickly it emerged.

Upon reflection, what I experienced is well known to the biblical writers, and to centuries of

Christ followers just like me. "A heart at peace gives life to the body, but envy rots the bones" (Proverbs 14:30). "Anger is cruel and fury overwhelming, but who can stand before jealousy?" (Proverbs 27:4). "The acts of the sinful nature are obvious: sexual immorality, impurity...hatred, discord, jealousy, fits of rage, selfish ambition..." (Galatians 5:19-21). The only One who can handle jealously in a godly manner is God – the One who is jealous for our love and attention above all other loves vying for our affection.

Jealousy is one of those ugly words we'd all prefer to be expunged from our vocabulary and experience. Like it's sibling envy and its cousin anger, jealousy is what ekes out of a heart that's not fully at peace, vulnerable to various alternatives to godly fondness. Jealously raises its head when we're not content with our own circumstances, and prefer another's to our own. Jealousy emerges when we're in a complaining spirit and desirous of what's seemingly out of reach. Jealousy reeks with a stench of disharmony from within and wreaks havoc on our walk with others.

In the Scriptures God shares with us poignant stories of jealousy. One of the premier stories is about the jealousy of Joseph's brothers toward their younger brother that grew into hatred when they saw how much their father loved him (Genesis 37:4). Or, King Saul's vengeance toward the young and successful warrior man David, toward whom he kept a jealous eye (1 Samuel 18:8).

In the New Testament we see jealousy emerge in two parables of Jesus. The first is the depiction of laborers hired to work in the vineyard, who were enraged with jealousy when they were paid the same wage as those who were hired in the last hour of the day (Matthew 20:12). Another such story is the parable of the prodigal son, and the response of the elder son to the extravagant ways the father displayed his love toward his wayward brother who had come to his senses and returned home once more (Luke 15: 28).

In what ways has your heart grown jealous recently? Is someone around you making more money, enjoying more happiness, expressing more delight, looking more beautiful, sounding more intelligent, owning more possessions, or appearing more athletic than you? If you're not able to celebrate their personal life circumstance, then perhaps there's a seed of jealousy burrowing it's head down deep in the soil of your heart. Left unattended, it's bound to grow into rage, dissension, factions and envy, or other less desirable responses.

Exploring the condition of our heart requires us to look authentically in the mirror of our attitudes toward others and within ourselves. Most likely, if you're experiencing jealousy, the invitation from God is to find your joy in him. "Rejoice with those who rejoice; mourn with those who mourn. Live in harmony with one another… if it is possible, as far as it depends on you, live at peace with everyone" (Romans 12: 15-18). And, learn the secret of contentment "whatever the circumstances…in need…in plenty…in any and every situation, whether well fed or hungry, whether living in plenty or in want. I can do everything through him who gives me strength" (Philippians 4: 11-13).

Day 10

Journal: Reflections on My Jealous Heart

_____

_____

_____

_____

_____

_____

_____

_____

_____

_____

_____

_____

_____

_____

_____

_____

_____

_____

_____

Day 12

The Forgiving Heart

If there's one word I'd like to not only have in my everyday vocabulary but also in the core of my heart's deepest desire, it's the word: forgiving. How I long to have a truly forgiving heart... but in certain circumstances and challenging relationships this isn't always the case. How about for you?

Over the years I have found comfort and instruction from those I respect who not only write about the topic of forgiveness, but have lived it too. When perplexed as to the best way to handle tough relational situations, and discerning the way forward is muddy at best, I look to the spiritual leadership of others who have trod the path before me. I hope these guides will be a source of encouragement and strength to you too.

One of my prayer mentors, Rueben Job, writes, "Forgiveness is a life-and-death matter because forgiveness lies at the very heart of Christian belief and practice. To remove forgiveness from our theology and practice is to tear the heart out of any hope of faithful Christian discipleship, and it is to drive a stake through the heart of Christian community...Forgiveness can never be taken lightly by those who consider their own need of forgiveness. The words of Jesus that we pray bind our need for forgiveness firmly to our willingness to forgive. Forgiveness is not only a preposterous gift; it is unbelievably difficult and costly. That is why we may talk about it easily and practice it with such difficulty."

From Corrie Ten Boom, "Forgiveness is the key which unlocks the door of resentment and the handcuffs of hatred. It breaks the chains of bitterness and the shackles of selfishness." Dallas Willard adds, "We forgive someone of a wrong they have done us when we decide that we will not make them suffer for it in any way."

Henri Nouwen asserts, "The authority of compassion is the possibility of man to forgive his brother, because forgiveness is only real for him who has discovered the weakness of his friends and the sins of his enemy in his own heart."

James Howell writes, "When Jesus taught the disciples to pray, he grabbed hold of vertical forgiveness, 'O Lord, forgive me, for I have sinned' and nailed it to horizontal forgiveness, '…as we forgive those who trespass against us,' two interrelated acts of forgiveness, forming a cross. Jesus not only taught about forgiveness. He became forgiveness. He makes forgiveness possible and real." (Matt. 6: 12, 14,15).

Wendy Wright wisely contributes, "That which is unforgiven holds us captive. We are imprisoned by the hatred and malice we clutch in our hearts… When wrongs have been committed the last thing one wants, or even should do, is claim that the transgression should be overlooked. It is a long and painful process to move through the stages of healing that must occur for forgiveness to begin. The injury must be named and claimed as part of you, the pain allowed to work for you, the injurer must rightly be blamed, and power and strength returned to the injured. Then, knowing you have experienced pain and overcome it, forgiveness can come as a free act. Forgiveness can be the great cleansing action that allows one to begin again."

Forgiveness is the turnkey to a loving heart. Forgiveness is the lynch pin to a gracious relationship. Forgiveness is the capstone of a godly life. Forgiveness is the evidence of a generous heart. Forgiveness is granted out of the depth of what is received…received with depth of appreciation, it will be delivered with a strength that comes from the well within. Forgiveness is at the heart of the gospel and remains at the heart of the One who declared it often, yes Jesus himself. To receive his outstretched arms of love is to offer such to all who cross our path, no matter how painful or costly or humbling it may be.

How will a forgiving heart toward others (even when it's not just forgiving them seven times, but seventy-seven times – Matt. 18: 22) lead you into freedom, fullness, and joy once more?

Day 12

Journal: Reflections on My Forgiving Heart

_____

_____

_____

_____

_____

_____

_____

_____

_____

_____

_____

_____

_____

_____

_____

_____

_____

_____

_____

Day 13

✺

The Hateful Heart

It's intriguing to note how often the word hate lands in the biblical text. Most of the references deal with what God hates (evil, falsehood, robbery, iniquity, wickedness, and even divorce). The Bible gets specific in Proverbs 6: 16-19 as, "Six things the Lord hates, seven that are detestable to him: haughty eyes, a lying tongue, hands that shed innocent blood, a heart that devises wicked schemes, feet that are quick to rush into evil, a false witness who pours out lies, and a man who stirs up dissension among brothers."

How much hate do you have for the things that God hates? Do you hate it when you have haughty pride in your eyes or when you see it in another?

Do you hate it when you find yourself glossing over the facts and spinning the story into a lie? Do you hate to see innocent lives taken by war, famine, or injustice? Do you hate it when you see how people are scheming to hurt another or avoid being held responsible for their inappropriate actions? Do you hate it when you see violence, bloodshed, or any form of evil? Do you hate it when false accounts, lies, and dissension are destroying communities, churches, families, or friendships? If so, then having hate toward the things that God hates is what leads to passionate compassion toward arresting ungodliness.

There are several passages in the Bible that speak about what we are to hate as God's people, summarized simply as evil and sinfulness. We're reminded as well that it is actually a blessing to be blasphemed by others for loving God, and in turn we are admonished to do good toward all who hate us. In other words, join God in hating all the things that he hates (see above) and learn to turn the other cheek toward all who hate you for loving God and godliness, instead of evil and hatred among people.

Turned even more horizontally, however, what about a God-fearing person who hates another God-fearing person? That's when it gets confusing. It's one thing to have a hateful heart as a non-believer, or to receive the hatred of a non-believer, but what about a hateful heart that exists within and among God's family? How can hate toward another Christian ever be justified?

"Anyone who claims to be in the light but hates his brother is still in the darkness. Whoever loves his brother lives in the light, and there is nothing in him to make him stumble. But whoever hates his brother is in the darkness and walks around in the darkness; he does not know where he is going, because the darkness has blinded him," writes John in 1 John 2: 9-11.

Whenever I hear a Christian describe a hateful heart toward another in the family of God I hear inner torment and unresolved anger. There's a blockage in the heart that stubbornly refuses to let any light shine on the hate that resides within. It's considered easier to carry around animosity, malice, and spite than to deal openly, honestly, and lovingly toward those we may hate. But, since the truth always sets us free, a hateful heart can indeed be healed by the presence and power of God. When confronted by the initiating love of the Father, Son, and Holy Spirit, a hateful heart can be melted away and replaced instead with mercy, grace, and joy.

"We love because he first loved us. If anyone says, 'I love God,' yet hates his brother, he is a liar. For anyone who does not love his brother, whom he has seen, cannot love God, whom he has not seen. And he has given us this command: Whoever loves God must also love his brother" (1 John 4: 19-21). Does any shred of hate reside in your heart today, toward God or one of God's people? Rid yourself of the weight that burdens your heart and instead find freedom to love as one who's been loved by God in order to love another.

Day 13

Journal: Reflections on My Hateful Heart

_____
_____
_____
_____
_____
_____
_____
_____
_____
_____
_____
_____
_____
_____
_____
_____
_____
_____
_____
_____

Day 14

The Hopeful Heart

Do you get to spend much time with a hopeful person? Someone who lives wisely, listens intently, and continuously pours life, courage, perspective, encouragement and confident expectancy into your soul? Contrast that with the person who seems to be constantly burdened by life, and regularly appears pessimistic, deflated, cynical, and ultimately quite hopeless. Most likely you prefer spending time with a hopeful heart… and long for that attitude yourself.

As we peruse the Scriptures for insights into the hopeful heart we soon discover that the majority of biblical references focus on pinning our hope on the God of hope. "May the God of hope fill you with all joy and peace as you trust in him, so that you may overflow with hope by the power of the Holy Spirit" (Romans 15:13).

God is the primary source of our hope. When we put our hope in God, we see him at work with growing clarity and conviction no matter the circumstances of our lives, "though he slay me, yet will I hope" (Job 13:15). "Put your hope in God" cries the psalmist (Psalm 42:5), for "my hope comes from him" (Psalm 62:5). When we put our trust completely in God's hands his plan is to "give us a hope and a future" (Jeremiah 29:11). Hope is an anchor for our soul (Hebrews 6:19) and our foundation of hope is found in God's Word, for "in his word I put my hope" (Psalm 119: 74; 130: 5).

When hope is at the center of our hearts, then we look with faith toward all of our tomorrows. We hope in God for a brighter future, where hope springs eternal and lifts our overburdened hearts to soaring potential over current circumstances. Hope is the fuel needed to keep moving forward. Hope is contagious when shared among the people of God in worship, word, and witness.

Without hope our hearts are arrested by current realities that can dishearten the hopeful and pull down even the most optimistic among us.

So what happens when hope is stolen from us? When rocks, weeds and thorns infiltrate the soil of our faith, and hope is robbed and replaced with counterfeit gods that seek to satisfy but always leave us hollow? "Hope deferred makes the heart sick" (Proverbs 13:12), so when hope is held at a distance the heart grows cold, hard, crushed, and devastated. Hope is easily swept away when hardship or disappointment disheartens and discourages the heart. Such hope "deferrals" come upon us suddenly while others creep in over time, and often unaware.

Hope isn't unbridled buoyancy or glassy-eyed optimism. Christian hope comes from the deep-seated conviction that God reigns supreme in every aspect of our lives. Despite the suffering and adversity of this world, we have every reason to cling to hope. The life, death, and resurrection of Christ is what fills our hearts with hope, both for the present and the future. With eternity in our hearts, we are filled to overflowing with hope.

Having witnessed God at work in your own heart, and observing him at work in the hearts of others, what are the reasons for your hope today? Count the many blessings that have come your way and notice how God is alive and at work in, through, and around you. By attending to God you are fixing your eyes on him. That's how hope is birthed and kept alive within your heart. Choose today to show your world the transformation that emerges from the hopeful heart of God.

On what or whom are you most hopeful today? As you pray, consider adding words of hope into your conversation with God. Invite him to grant you hope even amidst your most difficult challenge. Ask God to grant you a pure sense of hope, without expectation or want or foregone conclusion. Lean fully into hope and watch your heart and mind expand beyond what you could ask, dream or imagine today.

Day 14

Journal: Reflections on My Hopeful Heart

_____

_____

_____

_____

_____

_____

_____

_____

_____

_____

_____

_____

_____

_____

_____

_____

_____

_____

_____

_____

Day 15

❦

The Angry Heart

In the Old Testament, we read of instances when the Lord shows forth his anger toward his disobedient followers. When Moses was up on Mount Sinai listening to the Lord's instructions about The Sabbath, and receiving the two tablets of the Testimony, Aaron and the people grew impatient in their waiting. Instead, they took matters into their own hands and made a god for themselves in the form of a golden calf. Their stiff-necked action angered the Lord greatly, but Moses pleaded for them so they would not be destroyed, and the Lord relented (Exodus 32). Elsewhere, the Israelites wandered in the desert for forty years and did not see the land God had promised Abraham, Isaac and Jacob – except for Caleb and

Joshua who followed the Lord wholeheartedly – because the Lord's anger burned against their disobedience (Numbers 32).

However, the biblical text emphatically suggests that even God bridles his anger and is instead slow to anger and abounding in love, compassion, grace, faithfulness, mercy, and forgiveness. In Exodus 34, Moses proclaims this contrast, "The Lord, the Lord, the compassionate and gracious God, slow to anger, abounding in love and faithfulness, maintaining love to thousands, and forgiving wickedness, rebellion and sin." In Nehemiah 9:17, Nehemiah reiterates this same truth about God. Jonah, when he disobeyed God's instructions, and lands in the belly of a fish, comes forth with the testimony, "I knew that you are a gracious and compassionate God, slow to anger and abounding in love." David the psalmist joins the glad refrain in Psalms 86 and 103, "The Lord is compassionate and gracious, slow to anger, abounding in love. He will not always accuse, nor will he harbor his anger forever."

In the New Testament Jesus instructs his followers, "that anyone who is angry with his brother will be subject to judgment" (Matthew 5:22). Paul the apostle reminds the people of God that "love is not easily angered, it keeps no record of wrongs" (1 Cor. 13: 5) and "in your anger do not sin. Do not let the sun go down while you are still angry, and do not give the devil a foothold" (Eph. 4:26).

Anger is something that swells from a heart that's desirous of punishing another by expressing words, attitudes, and actions that ultimately hurt and potentially destroy. The Bible instructs us that anger is usually combined with hostility, strife and dissension. It's generally unleashed, aroused, burning, fierce, consumed, and harsh. It's rarely affirmed as productive toward any relationship. In fact, quite the opposite. "A fool gives full vent to his anger, but a wise man keeps himself under control" (Proverbs 29:11). And in clear analogies, "As churning the milk produces butter, and as twisting the nose produces blood, so stirring up anger produces strife" (Proverbs 30:33).

How then do we curb our anger and not let it consume our heart? If we don't want to let the sun go down on our anger or give the devil a foothold on our hearts and relationships with others, then how do we keep from sinning in the midst of our anger? The God-honoring, relationship-building answer: "Everyone should be quick to listen and slow to speak and slow to become angry, for man's anger does not bring about the righteous life that God desires" (James 1:19).

Quick to listen + Slow to speak = Slow to become angry. A simple equation to offer, but incredibly difficult to execute. Since most of our anger spews like lava from the hotbed of our troubled souls, it often feels impossible to contain. But, does it always have to come pouring out to burn and consume another? The passage in James suggests otherwise. Quick to listen...stop yourself, cease quarreling, restrain judgment, ask questions, empathetically listen. Slow to speak... hold your tongue, pause reflectively, ponder deeply, consider carefully, love graciously. Slow to become angry...hold back, reconsider, measure your words, monitor your tone of voice, watch your body language. An angry heart is an ugly heart. How will you monitor your anger today?

Day 15

Journal: Reflections on My Angry Heart

_____

_____

_____

_____

_____

_____

_____

_____

_____

_____

_____

_____

_____

_____

_____

_____

_____

_____

_____

_____

Day 16

❧

The Generous Heart

A generous hearted person understands that every resource we have in life comes from the gracious hand of Almighty God and is to be multiplied for Kingdom priorities and purposes. There is nothing that we own or steward that belongs fully to us, no matter how it was initially acquired. We enter this world with nothing in our hands but life itself, and we exit this world with nothing short of our final breath.

So why do we cling to the attachments of this world? An attachment to food can lead to gluttony. An attachment to passion can lead to lust. An attachment to winning can lead to bullying. An attachment to resources can lead to selfishness. An attachment to power can lead to manipulation. An attachment to our capabilities can lead to pride. An attachment to liberalities can lead to anarchy. An attachment to chemical substances can lead to addiction.

The abundant life we're invited into by Jesus requires a healthy detachment from the things of this world so that our hearts can fully attach to the heart of Christ. Only then will we know what inner contentment looks and feels like. Only then will we live a life of true joy, harmony, justice, continuity, effectiveness, faithfulness, obedience, sacrifice, mercy, and love. The abundant life of the Christ follower is experienced when we prayerfully make God's priorities our daily priorities.

Jesus makes this profoundly clear in John 12: 23-26, "The hour has come for the Son of Man to be glorified. I tell you the truth, unless a kernel of wheat falls to the ground and dies, it remains only a single seed. But if it dies, it produces many seeds. The man who loves his life will lose it, while the man who hates his life in this world will keep it for eternal life. Whoever serves me must follow me; and where I am, my servant also will

be. My Father will honor the one who serves me."
The amazing paradox of this passage is contained
in three insights: only by death comes life; only by
spending life do we retain it; and only by service
comes greatness.

In other words, it is only as we give that we
genuinely receive. It is when we have sacrificed
that we truly understand the fruitful blessing of
the cross. It is when we die to ourselves, our own
selfish ambitions, and our personal possessions,
that we recover the true meaning of joy. When
we fully understand the importance of sacrifice,
we live generously for God's glory and another's
good.

Generosity is fulfilled tangibly and intangibly.
Tangible generosity is evidenced in sharing what
we have with another – our financial resources,
and the things we have been able to purchase and
acquire in this world. Intangible generosity is in
the time we're willing to share with another in
need of friendship or companionship, counsel or
compassion. Intangible generosity is seen in the
use of our gifts and talents in service to others
and to the glory of God. It also is expressed

in the hospitality of the soul toward another – in listening attentively, loving graciously, learning wholeheartedly, and living sacrificially. Generosity is best typified by the contrast between an open hand of generous stewardship with the closed hand of stingy control.

A generous heart knows with certainty that God prospers us not to raise our standard of living, but to raise our standard of giving. Unless a kernel of wheat falls to the ground and dies, it remains only a single seed. Therefore, detach from your kernels of possession (your time, talent and treasure) with an open hand of generosity toward Kingdom priorities and purposes, and then watch them reap a multiplied harvest more than you could ever ask, dream or imagine. It is in giving that we receive...so what do you have in your hand that needs to be let go, fall to the ground and die today?

God loves a cheerful and generous giver. He is one himself, and he invites us to be one too. Will you?

Day 16

Journal: Reflections on My Generous Heart

_____

_____

_____

_____

_____

_____

_____

_____

_____

_____

_____

_____

_____

_____

_____

_____

_____

_____

_____

Day 17

❧

The Prideful Heart

First and best and most important. That was the request of James and John, the sons of Zebedee, when they came to Jesus with the bold request, "Teacher," they said, "we want you to do for us whatever we ask." When Jesus asked them to clarify their appeal, they replied, "Let one of us sit at your right and the other at your left in your glory." (Mark 10: 35-45). When Jesus asked them a follow up question about being able to drink the cup or be baptized with what he was about to be baptized with (his pending cross and crucifixion), they foolishly and naively replied "yes we can." They obviously didn't know what they were saying!

When the other ten disciples heard about their incredible desire for being considered first and best and most important in glory, they were indignant with James and John. Jesus calmed them down with a simple reminder, "Whoever wants to become great among you must be your servant, and whoever wants to be first must be slave of all" (vs. 43, 44).

The prideful heart pursues being first, best and most important...rarely considering the position of second, least, or last. The pride of the sovereign self places your own interests paramount to all others. Pride is thinking of yourself as more important than others, better than others, or above others because of your name, achievements, gifts, looks, knowledge, possessions, or wealth. A prideful heart is self-exalted over others and becomes offended when people don't give you the attention, respect, or honor you think you deserve. When a person considers self above others, then selfish ambition and vain conceit reign supreme. Pride and arrogance – an overly inflated sense of your own importance – ultimately breeds quarrels, dissension, and animosity.

The Bible speaks often of the self-righteous, self-sufficient, and self-indulgent, and is clear about God hating pride as one of seven abominations noted in Proverbs 6. In Proverbs 18:12 we are reminded of the fruit of pride, "Pride goes before a fall, but humility comes before honor." And both James 4:6 and 1 Peter 5:5 quote Proverbs 29:3-4, which says, "God opposes the proud but gives grace to the humble."

Pride is continually contrasted in the Scriptures with humility and wisdom. A prideful heart is rarely teachable or hospitable, nor does one see the value of empathic listening or compassionate concern. However, these are the very words that break the bondage of pride: humility, wisdom, hospitality, listening, and compassion. If you think you're immune to pride, think again. It resides in your heart and it shows its ugly head more times than you care to admit. Are you willing to acknowledge and address your own pride today? When does your pride emerge and what is God inviting you to consider in response?

A prideful heart is one that's focused on self-aggrandizement, self-referencing, and self-protection. Pride puffs up and makes sure they are seen and heard above all others. Pride quickly gives voice to ones gifts, abilities, experiences, wisdom, wit, and opinion before even considering the need to listen to another. Pride makes sure one is protected from the fiery darts of others who are offensive, threatening, or belittling. Pride is the sign of deep insecurities that can only be broken by the conviction of the Spirit and the honesty of a friend.

When Jesus reminded James , John and the other disciples about how pride is conquered he called them to a life of servanthood. And, he offered them his humble self an example worthy of a following, "For even the Son of Man did not come to be served but to serve, and to give his life as a ransom for many" (Mark 10: 45). The antidote to a prideful heart is a servant's heart. Being willing to serve another, even without notice, is a wonderful way to rid you of pride and consider others more important than yourself. May that be your choice of your heart today.

Day 17

Journal: Reflections on My Prideful Heart

_____

_____

_____

_____

_____

_____

_____

_____

_____

_____

_____

_____

_____

_____

_____

_____

_____

_____

_____

_____

Day 18

❧

The Compassionate Heart

A compassionate heart comes from a transformed heart…one that's been changed from the inside out. Upon receiving the love, grace, mercy, and forgiveness of God, the overflow is compassion toward others. Compassion is a deep awareness of the suffering of another accompanied by an earnest desire to bring relief. It's that feeling of pity and distress over the suffering or misfortune of another and the effort to help alleviate it.

Our family supports Compassion International, a child sponsorship relief and development agency that's doing amazing work worldwide. This organization brings out the sympathetic consciousness of Christian men and women who share a common desire to bear the burdens of those much less fortunate than we are today. In supporting Compassion we in turn are coming alongside children and their families in impoverished nations around the globe. There are many other groups like Compassion, such as World Relief and World Vision, who share such a mission of compassionate mercy. Each ministry extends compassion to the lost and least of these who suffer physically, mentally, and spiritually, and do so with godly integrity.

This kind of co-suffering (the Latin root of compassion) comes from our emotional or passionate response to "do unto others what you would have them do to you" which is the Golden Rule (Matthew 7:12). When we are compelled to serve others compassionately, we do so with empathy for the pain, heartache, and disappointment caused by suffering of all forms and magnitudes. A compassionate heart is able to reach beyond one's personal needs or interests and into the life of another, doing so in ways that we would appreciate receiving if ever in a similar situation.

Jesus' Parable of the Good Samaritan (Luke 10: 25-37) is an expression of true compassion shown indiscriminately to all in need, and is in keeping with Jesus' Sermon on the Mount, "Blessed are the merciful, for they shall obtain mercy." In the parable it was "the one who had mercy on him" who shows us how to be a neighbor to another in need. The priest and Levite passed by the man who had been beaten by robbers, but the Samaritan took pity on him, bandaged his wounds, poured oil on him, put the man on his donkey, took him to the inn and cared for him out of his own financial resources. The Samaritan had a compassionate heart and his alleviation of suffering brings a smile to the face of God.

The Apostle Paul commends the Church in Corinth to live out the compassion of God toward one another. "Praise be to the God and Father of our Lord Jesus Christ, the Father of compassion and the God of all comfort, who comforts us in all our troubles, so that we can comfort those in any trouble with the comfort we ourselves have received from God" (2 Corinthians 1: 3-4). The Scriptures are filled with references to the Father of compassion who continually shows mercy, love and compassion to his beloved children.

Jesus expressed compassion every place he traveled and served. Each of his miracles was offered out of compassion to the situation and people involved. His willingness to call out and come alongside his disciples is an example of compassion. His work of physical and emotional healing, casting out demons, providing food for the hungry, freeing those in bondage to sin, forgiving the sinner, reconciling family members, even weeping for a friend, were all examples of Jesus' life of compassionate love. He always went the extra mile, turned the other cheek, and in so doing captured the hearts of his followers. What would Jesus do if he were me? – is a great question to ask when confronted by the obvious need to show compassion.

Identify those in your sphere of influence who are in need of compassion and comfort today. Who do you know who's alone, in prison, hurting, hungry, and/or suffering in body, mind, or spirit?

In what ways can you prayerfully, lovingly and tangibly express compassion today? May your compassionate heart overflow toward all who you know are in need, and may the God of all comfort envelop and sustain you in your acts of merciful service now and always. Amen.

Day 18

Journal: Reflections on My Compassionate Heart

_____
_____
_____
_____
_____
_____
_____
_____
_____
_____
_____
_____
_____
_____
_____
_____
_____
_____
_____
_____

Day 19

❦

The Rebellious
Heart

Simply put, the rebellious heart says "No" to God. When we stiff-arm God, ignore his commandments, turn a deaf ear to his voice, and take matters into our own hands, we show forth our rebellion. One may consider a rebellious heart as only residing in a wicked person. But, in actuality, all of us experience our own form of rebellion during the years or seasons when we turned away from or refused to acknowledge God. And, in those random times when we stand fast in our prideful place and purposefully or inadvertently walk away from God in either heart, mind and/or action.

In the biblical text we see examples of the rebellious heart both in the life of the unbeliever and in the follower of God. In Isaiah we find this warning, "Woe to the obstinate children, to those who carry out plans that are not mine, forming an alliance, but not by my Spirit, heaping sin upon sin" (Isaiah 30:1). He describes the rebellious with these words, "These are rebellious people, deceitful children, children unwilling to listen to the Lord's instruction…Tell us pleasant things, prophesy illusions. Leave this way, get off this path, and stop confronting us with the Holy One of Israel!" (Isaiah 30: 9-11).

In 1 Samuel 15 we learn about King Saul's human condition. He was more concerned about man-pleasing than he was about serving God. He selectively obeyed some of God's commands and manipulated others to fit his own desires. Because of his disobedient and rebellious heart, God removed his kingship. In defending his actions, Saul's true heart was exposed by Samuel, "To obey is better than sacrifice, and to heed is better than the fat of rams, for rebellion is like the sin of divination, and arrogance like the evil of idolatry. Because you have rejected the word of the Lord, he has rejected you as king" (1 Samuel 15: 22,23). Saul's rebellion was paralleled to witchcraft, and his imperfections are in stark contrast to King David who was a man after God's heart, despite his many imperfections.

Ultimately, it's one's rejection of the Word of God that kindles a rebellious heart. "If anyone turns a deaf ear to the law, even his prayers are detestable" (Proverbs 28:9). In other words, the prayers of a rebellious heart are an abomination to the Lord. This is one of the harshest words God uses to describe an action that he hates. But, consider why...if you turn your heart against God and against his Word, how would you have the audacity to pray to the very God you rebel against? Isaiah's remedy to our rebellion? "This is what the Sovereign Lord, the Holy One of Israel says: in repentance and rest is your salvation, in quietness and trust is your strength" (Isaiah 30:15).

A rebellious heart refuses to repent. But, only in repentance and rest will a rebel find salvation. When a rebellious heart is open to God and willing to come clean before the Lord, then the loving Father welcomes that child home with a generous, eternal embrace. And that's exactly what happens to the rebellious younger son in Luke 15. As the rebellious prodigal son comes to his senses and turns back home, the prodigal (another word for extravagant) God runs his direction to offer an embrace, a kiss, a robe, a ring, new sandals, and a party to celebrate his repentance and renewed trust in God.

"What shall we say, then? Shall we go on sinning so that grace may increase? By no means! We died to sin; how can we live in it any longer?" (Romans 6: 1,2). Is it time for you to reconsider the rebellious corners of your heart, where darkness and sin may reside? "Thanks be to God that, though you used to be slaves to sin, you wholeheartedly obeyed the form of teaching to which you were entrusted. You have been set free from sin and have become slaves to righteousness" (Romans 6: 17, 18). Confess those parts of you that reflect a rebellious heart and be set free to surrender into the fullness of eternal life in Christ Jesus our Lord!

Day 19

Journal: Reflections on My Rebellious Heart

_____

_____

_____

_____

_____

_____

_____

_____

_____

_____

_____

_____

_____

_____

_____

_____

_____

_____

_____

Day 20

The Thoughtful Heart

"Be careful what you think, your thoughts run your life" (Proverbs 4:23, The New Century Version). This same verse is translated by the NIV as "Guard your heart, for it's the wellspring of life." Heartfelt thoughtfulness is likened to the inner source of strength for the vitality of our lives...out of which pours forth blessing, honor, grace, peace, encouragement and love. The Bible is replete with examples of how a thoughtful heart pleases God and empowers others. What is the litany of thoughts that are resident deep within the condition of your heart today?

In one of his concluding admonitions, the Apostle Paul urges the Church in Philippi with this clear exhortation, "Finally, brothers and sisters, whatever is true, whatever is noble, whatever is right, whatever is pure, whatever is lovely, whatever is admirable—if anything is excellent or praiseworthy—think about such things" (Phil. 4:8). These eight attributes of a thoughtful heart are worthy of our consideration as well.

1. True: all that's agreeable to the unchangeable, eternal truth, both in God's Word and in the natural world.
2. Noble: whatever is honest, grave, or venerable in speech, in contrast to levity and frivolity that withholds integrity.
3. Right: that which is just between two individuals and in relationship between God and humankind, in opposition to injustice, violence and oppression.
4. Pure: whatsoever is virtuous in word and deed, in agreement with the will of God and promotes holiness of heart and life.
5. Lovely: that which cultivates and increases love, friendship, and cordiality among individuals, and which is lovely in the sight of God.

6. Admirable: of good report, well spoken of, which leads to a name and a reputation, which is precious, respectful, kind and virtuous.
7. Excellent: the virtue of promoting the general good of all, with outstanding merit, gracefulness, and godly intent.
8. Praiseworthy: deserving commendation by others due to the stewardship and generosity offered to all who cross one's path.

A thoughtful heart considers ways to fan into flame these eight attributes, all of which contribute to the health of the body and the expansion of the kingdom of God. When righteousness and holiness dominate our thoughts, then our hearts and lives are expressed in agreement with the seeds planted in our minds. The most thoughtful people in our lives believe the best of God for the totality of our days, and pour courage into our hearts as a result. Choose thoughtfulness toward others and think about these things, letting them penetrate the deepest recesses of your spiritual mind and activate the richest charity toward others.

A person who embodies thoughtfulness is one who is considered wise among his peers. A thoughtful person doesn't speak unless there is something meaningful to offer. A thoughtful person will ponder the significance of events, relationships, opinions, attitudes, and actions, and will consider the various angles of each. Thoughtfulness is an attribute of the heart and the mind combined together to form a delightful way of being present in this world, within one's self, and among others.

When the believer in Jesus Christ both practices and recommends these eight thoughtful exhortations, then the heart of the gospel of Jesus Christ is fulfilled through the heart of the Church, for the sake of the heart of another, and for the expansion of the Kingdom of God here on earth. The thoughtful heart is a true reflection of God's heart, forever considerate of our best interests and our greatest needs. Will this become your prayer and the choice of your will as well?

Day 20

Journal: Reflections on My Thoughtful Heart

_____

_____

_____

_____

_____

_____

_____

_____

_____

_____

_____

_____

_____

_____

_____

_____

_____

_____

_____

_____

Day 21

The Selfish Heart

A selfish-hearted person is someone who thinks first and foremost of self. Referred to as self-referencing, self-aggrandizing, or self-absorption, such a person can hardly see beyond oneself. Consumed by self-consideration, such a person can only find satisfaction when their needs are placed at the front of the line. Selfishness is defined as placing concern with oneself or one's own interests, benefits or welfare above the well-being or regardless of the interests of others. Synonyms include egocentric, parsimonious, self-centered, self-indulgent, self-interested, self-seeking, wrapped up in oneself. It's the opposite of unselfish, caring and kind. Narcissism is a modern form of excessive or exclusive selfishness.

However, no matter the label, the manifestation isn't pretty to all who surround, observe, and are affected by such a person.

God's opinion of selfishness is crystal clear. It is an act of the sinful nature (Galatians 5:19-21). It is present wherever disorder and evil is practiced (James 3: 16, 17). It is harbored alongside bitter envy in the heart (James 3: 13-15). It is the opposite of love and humility and contradicts the very heart of God. Instead of selfishness, believers are urged by the Apostle Paul, "If you have any encouragement from being united with Christ, if any comfort from his love, if any fellowship with the Spirit, if any tenderness and compassion, then make my joy complete by being like-minded, having the same love, being one in spirit and purpose. Do nothing out of selfish ambition or vain conceit, but in humility consider others better than yourselves. Each of you should look not only to your own interests, but also to the interests of others" (Philippians 2: 1-4).

Do nothing out of selfish ambition – those are strong words indeed. Nothing? Yes, nada, says God.

Imagine a life without selfishness. Is it possible? In a world filled with self-everything, can we begin to make a dent in this reality? Only God's Spirit can make such a crevice in our heart, separating self from godliness, beginning first in the internal fibers of our being and extending outward into our words, attitudes, and actions.

If the fruit of the Spirit (love, joy, peace, patience, kindness, goodness, faithfulness, gentleness, and self-control) is to be evidenced in our hearts and lives, we must lean fully on the Spirit. We cannot break out of our self-centeredness without the Spirit of God residing in our hearts. The selfish heart can only be healed, restored, and redeemed by the presence and power of the Holy Spirit.

Therefore, the only place where it's legitimate to be selfish is in the opening up of ourselves to receive God's Spirit, his love, Word, and power. Finding the time and space to become attentive to God, noticing God, and receiving God is the largest, most looming need of the heart. Pressing the pause button of our fast-paced, me-centered lives and resting in the arms of Almighty God is the greatest comfort we can pursue. Anything less than that is an idol of our selfish heart.

Selfishness can suffocate the heart. And the heart needs to breathe in order to properly function. The oxygen of the heart is what keeps it pumping out and offering life to another. Selfish thoughts, selfish attitudes, selfish words, and selfish actions all combine to create a self-absorbed heart. Be selfish only as it relates to the care and nurture of your soul. Do this and God will break your selfishness and reveal to you infinite ways to give of yourself to another, to others, and to countless more throughout your lifetime.

So what will you do today to put your selfish heart into the hands of God, to mold and shape and transform you into a person who reflects God's heart? Turn your heart toward home, which is the beautiful heart of God...and in prayerful trust, become God's instrument of tenderness, compassion, and humility toward all who cross your path this and every new day.

Day 21

Journal: Reflections on My Selfish Heart

_____

_____

_____

_____

_____

_____

_____

_____

_____

_____

_____

_____

_____

_____

_____

_____

_____

_____

_____

_____

Day 22

❦

The Caring Heart

One of my dearest friends called recently to say how thankful he is for our relationship. Within ten minutes of that call an email arrived from a colleague expressing heartfelt gratitude for helping her with a recent teaching opportunity. Earlier in the day we were served by a small group of beloved saints who offered their time and talent in our behalf. What did each person have in common? They cared enough to express their love in tangible and intangible ways. Their care-full-ness was and remains a gift I will treasure deeply and with all my heart. Like the card company who coined the phrase, they too "cared enough to send the very best." Their very best was their caring selves.

A caring heart is affectionate, helpful, and sympathetic toward someone or something that's important to be concerned about. Those who serve in a caring profession express their care tangibly and attentively toward another, as a nurse, social worker, counselor, pastor, and/or physician might do. They "take care" to follow up on words with actions which embody and fulfill their care-giving. Likewise as believers, when invited to cast our cares upon God, we are urged to bring our worries, concerns, anxieties or fears to the One who desires to attend to them lovingly in our behalf. Whether by God or one of his emissaries, a caring heart is always a balm for our souls and is to be received as if they are the very arms and voice of God. Who among us doesn't have such a need each day?

Nestled within The Great Commandment (Matthew 22: 37: loving God with heart, soul, mind and strength) and The Great Commission (Matthew 28: 19,20: as we go, making disciples of all nations) is what some would describe as The Great Compassion. It's found in Matthew 25: 35, 36, "Come, you who are blessed by my Father; take your inheritance, the kingdom prepared for you since the creation of the world. For I was hungry and you gave me something to eat, I was thirsty and you gave me something to drink, I was a stranger and you invited me in, I needed clothes and you clothed me, I was sick and you looked after me, I was in prison and you came to visit me."

In Jesus' understanding of a caring heart the hungry are fed, the thirsty are given drink, the stranger is welcomed, the needy are clothed, the sick are attended, and the imprisoned are visited. Thus his admonition in Matthew 25: 40, "I tell you the truth, whatever you did for one of the least of these brothers of mine, you did for me." A caring heart not only serves those within our reach, but more importantly to those who are less likely to be on our radar screen…the least, the lost, the lonely, the last, and the left behind. Those who care enough to serve the impoverished are known as sheep by the Good Shepherd, but those who ignore the needy are separated out as goats that are destined to eternal punishment.

In the gospels we read many stories of loving and caring hearts being expressed toward those in need. One of the most vivid is when a paralytic is being carried by his friends on a mat to lay him before Jesus to be healed. But when they noticed the crowd with Jesus was too large to enter the house, the stretcher bearers hoisted him up onto the roof and then proceeded to lower him on his mat through the roof tiles and into the middle of the crowd, right in front of Jesus (Luke 5: 17-20). Their heroism of helpfulness came forth from their helpful and caring hearts. When Jesus saw *their* faith, he said, "Friend, your sins are forgiven" and in that moment the presence and power of the Lord was offered to the paralytic, the faith of his friends was strengthened, and "everyone was amazed and gave praise to God. They were filled with awe and said, 'We have seen remarkable things today'" (Luke 5: 26).

Blessed is the one who has a caring heart, and then acts upon it empathetically toward another. It's one thing to consider a caring action and another thing altogether to act upon such an intuition. A caring heart both feels for a person or lives a principled life, and then puts feet to those emotive responses with words and actions in support of another. Who around you or within your reach is in need of your caring heart? How will you express your care-full-ness today?

Day 22

Journal: Reflections on My Caring Heart

_____

_____

_____

_____

_____

_____

_____

_____

_____

_____

_____

_____

_____

_____

_____

_____

_____

_____

_____

Day 23

❧

The Discriminating Heart

Our God does not show partiality or favoritism, and neither should we (Deut. 10: 17-19). Created in the image and likeness of God (Genesis 1: 26, 27), all mankind is to be treated without bias or prejudice. Instead of discriminating as judges with evil thoughts toward those who are different from us, we are called to love all of our neighbors as we love ourselves (John 13: 34).

Racism in varying forms and various degrees has been a part of the human condition since the dawn of time.

This social ill has been a struggle among family groups, between ethnicities, and across religious, political, cultural and socioeconomic backgrounds for generations. Victims of bigotry, hatred, and intolerance have been judged and tainted in the hearts of others, including those who claim the name of Christ as Lord. The Bible is clear about this issue and there is little we can dismiss as inappropriate for our own place and time in history.

God so loved the world – every ethnic group on planet earth – that he gave his only begotten Son to lay down his life for us (John 3: 16).

Jesus, the great reconciler, invites his followers to be united in him and lovers of one another. "Do not judge, or you too will be judged," Jesus teaches in Matthew 7:1, 2, "For in the same way you judge others, you will be judged, and with the measure you use, it will be measured to you." Peter has a vision and preaches to the early church at Cornelius' home about this same topic, "God does not show favoritism but accepts men from every nation who fear him and do what is right" (Acts 10: 34, 35). The Apostle Paul picks up on this same topic in his ministry to the body of Christ,

"Do not think of yourself more highly than you ought, but rather think of yourself with sober judgment, in accordance with the measure of faith God has given you" (Romans 12: 3). And to the Galatians, "There is neither Jew nor Greek, slave nor free, male nor female, for you are all one in Christ Jesus" (Galatians 3:28).

In James 2: 1-26 this theme is highlighted in the form of favoritism, specifically between economic distinctions, "Don't show favoritism. Suppose a man comes into your meeting wearing a gold ring and fine clothes, and a poor man in shabby clothes also comes in. If you show special attention to the man wearing fine clothes and say, 'Here's a good seat for you,' but you say to the poor man, 'You stand there,' or 'Sit on the floor by my feet,' have you not discriminated among yourselves and become judges with evil thoughts?"

No matter where we turn in the Scriptures to enlighten our hearts and minds on this subject, there is an accompanying mandate to act in accordance with God's priorities. Nowhere do we find God choosing favorites, showing bias against, preferring one over another, or speaking intolerantly toward those he created in his image. Discriminating against any person created in the image of God is simply not appropriate at any time or for any reason. Bigotry and prejudice and preferential treatment does not belong in the Church now or ever. As believers in the Lord Jesus Christ, we must take the lead in speaking up for any and all victims of discrimination.

Today our world is filled with hateful prejudice and judgmental partiality. Our biases toward those we agree with and against those with whom we differ deters the unity God desires among his people. Those who participate in any form of prejudice or partiality need to repent and seek forgiveness. This is where the truth of the gospel is practiced most specifically. Are you willing to admit that your heart at times discriminates against another? Do you see the log in your own eye, while looking so harshly at the speck in someone else's eye? For what offense of prejudicial accusation must you seek forgiveness? Your holy boldness of love, confession, and affirmation toward those you've wronged in your heart will lead to the freedom to serve and bless others like never before. Be free, dear friend!

Journal: Reflections on My Discriminating Heart

_____

_____

_____

_____

_____

_____

_____

_____

_____

_____

_____

_____

_____

_____

_____

_____

_____

_____

Day 24

⁓

The Joyful Heart

J oy is such a beautiful word, three simple letters tied together with gladness and enchantment. The word joy is defined as the emotion evoked by well-being, success, or good fortune or by the prospect of possessing what one desires; a state of happiness or contentment caused by something exceptionally good or satisfying; a source or cause of keen pleasure or delight; the expression or display of glad feeling or great appreciation. It's historic use is paired with terms such as rejoice, jubilation, exhilaration and triumph.

From a distinctly Christian perspective, to possess a joyful heart is to express a gift and empowerment from God. Joy is a fruit of God's

Spirit (Gal. 5:22), an evidence of the Lord's presence and power bursting forth from the deepest place of one's soul. To have a joyful and glad heart is to be grateful for the many gifts and blessings that come to us directly from the generous hand of God. It's seen throughout the Bible in the contexts of singing for joy, feasting with joy, comfort and joy, peace and joy, progress and joy, joy in hope, and shouts of joy.

Within the community of faith, the Apostle Paul reminds his beloved followers to put love into action by hating what is evil, clinging to what is good, being devoted to one another, honoring each other with sincere love. In so doing, to also "Be joyful in hope, patient in affliction, faithful in prayer" (Romans 12: 9-12). Joy is to be exhibited within the relationships we are invited to build for the glory of God. A joyful heart evokes joy among the Church and leads others into harmony with one another where we indeed rejoice with those who rejoice (and weep with those who weep). Joy is the glue that bonds our love together as children of the King.

However, joy isn't just for the positive times - it's more powerful when experienced in the darkest, most difficult times of life. "Consider it pure joy, my brothers and sisters, whenever you face trials of many kinds, because you know that the testing of your faith produces perseverance. Let perseverance finish its work so that you may be mature and complete, not lacking anything" (James 1: 2-4). No matter the circumstances of our lives, we are to rejoice and be glad. "Then I would still have this consolation – my joy in unrelenting pain – that I had not denied the words of the Holy One," testifies Job (Job 6:10). And from the Prophet Habakkuk, "Though the fig tree does not bud and there are no grapes on the vines, though the olive crop fails and the fields produce no food, though there are no sheep in the pen and no cattle in the stalls, yet I will rejoice in the Lord, I will be joyful in God my Savior. The Sovereign Lord is my strength; he makes my feet like the feet of a deer, he enables me to tread on the heights" (Hab. 3: 17-19).

Choosing and discovering joy in the midst of life's most trying obstacles and disappointments is nothing short of a miracle of God's grace. Having been in such a state many times in my Christian life, I have marveled at God's goodness and mercy over and over again. Though others may turn against me and cause me great harm; though loved ones may suffer untold agony of heart and body; though the world and the enemy of my soul may wreak havoc on the work of my hands...the Lord's faithfulness has turned my sorrow into joy and in that truth my heart is glad. We may not see the redemptive value of the pain we're in immediately, but in God's timing and through God's means his will radiates above and beyond the deepest heartache and suffering we endure this side of heaven. And we can sing with the prophet, "Yet I will rejoice in the Lord, I will be joyful in God my Savior!"

Since the Lord our God is always with us, taking great delight in us, rejoicing over us with singing (Zeph. 3:17), in response we too are to find our greatest joy in Him. The Apostle Paul urges the Thessalonians, "Rejoice always, pray continually, give thanks in all circumstances, for this is God's will for you in Christ Jesus" (1 Thess. 5: 16-18). Will you make that concerted choice and allow joy to be the posture of your heart, mind and will even today?

Day 24

Journal: Reflections on My Joyful Heart

_____

_____

_____

_____

_____

_____

_____

_____

_____

_____

_____

_____

_____

_____

_____

_____

_____

_____

_____

_____

Day 25

❧

The Closed Heart

Whenever you hear phrases such as "I will never..." or "I absolutely refuse..." or "There's simply no way..." no doubt there's a closed heart standing behind those words. Accompanying such words are attitudes that are closed, opposed, or negatively disposed against a person, concept, or suggestion. A closed heart is usually a reflection of a closed mind, which in turn is a depiction of a life that believes it knows more than others, has thought through a conviction to its "right" conclusion, or simply knows how best to feel under the circumstance. As a result, there is little one can say or do to penetrate the blockade that barricades one from even considering a new or different way. A closed heart is impenetrable even from the wisest, softest, wittiest, or clearest alternative.

Jesus quotes from Isaiah in describing one with a closed heart, "For this people's heart has become calloused; they hardly hear with their ears, and they have closed their eyes. Otherwise they might see with their eyes, hear with their ears, understand with their hearts and turn, and I would heal them" (Matthew 13: 15). This same principle from Isaiah is quoted by Paul in Acts 28:27 as he preached boldly about the kingdom of God to both closed and open hearts. In describing the wicked, the psalmist writes, "They close up their callous hearts, and their mouths speak with arrogance" (Psalm 17:10). This description is in sharp contrast to being known by God as "the apple of his eye" (Psalm 17: 8), one who is willing to have God probe and examine the heart, and ensure its openness to the wonder of God's great love.

An open heart is simply more pliable in consideration of alternative ways to think, feel and/or act. The polar opposite of a closed heart is an enormously wide open heart, one that can be in danger of being so open as to be non-sensible or extremely liberal. However, a healthy open heart is one that's balanced with perspective from a variety of vantage points and multiple voices. This kind of open heart is desirous of wisdom and perception that grows out of listening carefully to all sides before choosing one to follow. An open heart is the antidote to the rigidity, inflexibility, and intolerance which often follows the person who demonstrates a cold, calculating, and sometimes cruel closed heart. One thing is for certain: God opposes the pride of the closed heart, and seeks to gently open such a heart to receive fully the love, joy, peace, and hope of the gospel.

When we are open to receive from God and others, we in turn become open to becoming our full, true selves. Openness is an attribute that grows out of a teachable heart, one that wants to remain malleable in the hands of the Almighty One. Like soft, supple clay in the hands of our Maker, the Potter of our souls, we are formed, conformed and transformed more and more into his likeness. Openness to God and one another is depicted visually in the out-stretched arms of love displayed for us by Christ on the cross. His openness to his Father's will and way led Jesus from heaven into the womb of the virgin Mary, among people he could serve sacrificially and generously even to the cross, and eventually through the empty tomb of the resurrection and back to glory forever. God chose to send his Son into this world so that the alternatives of our choice for the God we serve would be made clear. Jesus' openness to the Father and the Spirit all throughout his earthly ministry is an abundant testimony to the gift that an open heart can be to all whom we are called to serve in Jesus' name.

In Philippi, a businesswoman by the name of Lydia, a dealer in purple cloth from the city of Thyatira, became a worshiper of God. "The Lord opened her heart to respond to Paul's message" after which members of her household joined her in the waters of baptism and practiced hospitality to Paul and his team (Acts 16: 13-15). Her openness to the Lord transformed her into a woman of devout worship and generous hospitality. Lydia is a great example for all who follow Christ and desire to remain open to his leading hand through the presence and power of his Spirit. This type of genuine conversion of heart is found embedded in Paul's prayer for the Ephesians, "I pray also that the eyes of your heart may be enlightened in order that you may know the hope to which he has called you, the riches of his glorious inheritance in the saints, and his incomparably great power for us who believe" (Eph. 1: 18, 19).

More than any other tangible instrument that opens a closed heart is the Word of God. Likewise, more than any other intangible means of grace that opens a closed heart is prayer. In the masterpiece Psalm 119, we read "Open my eyes that I may see wonderful things in your law" (verse 18). This verse combines the Word with prayer, so that the Law of God, his instruction and teaching, can profoundly elicit holiness in the heart of the believer. Without the empowerment of God's Holy Spirit we can only see what the natural eye can fathom. So, it's incumbent upon us to seek the gracious illumination of the Word and the Spirit to open up our closed heart so we can earnestly seek him with all our heart. An open Bible needs an open heart. Will you remain open to the fresh, renewing, heart-changing gospel today?

Day 25

Journal: Reflections on My Closed Heart

_____

_____

_____

_____

_____

_____

_____

_____

_____

_____

_____

_____

_____

_____

_____

_____

_____

_____

_____

_____

Day 26

The Pure Heart

"Blessed are the pure in heart, for they will see God," Jesus shares from the Mount of Beatitudes (Matthew 5:8). In this profound thought, Jesus is urging his listeners to remain pure in their heart and mind, for only in that condition will one be able to see, hear, and truly know God. The psalmists of old cry out in similar fashion, "The fear of the Lord is pure, enduring forever" (Psalm 19:9) and "He who has clean hands and a pure heart will receive blessing from the Lord and vindication from God his Savior" (Psalm 24: 4,5).

One of the purest stories in the biblical text is revealed between Elizabeth and Mary, as they are both carrying children in their womb who would later enter and envelop the world who longed for their coming. Classic Advent texts, we read in Luke 1 about Mary visiting her cousin Elizabeth, "When Elizabeth heard Mary's greeting, the baby leaped in her womb, and Elizabeth was filled with the Holy Spirit. In a loud voice she exclaimed, 'Blessed are you among women, and blessed is the child you will bear!'" (vs. 41,42). Mary's reply is one of worship and adoration, giving homage to her God, "My soul glorifies the Lord and my spirit rejoices in God my Savior, for his has been mindful of the humble state of his servant...the Mighty One has done great things for me – holy is his name...his mercy extends to those who fear him...he has performed mighty deeds...he has scattered the proud...he has filled the hungry with good things" (Luke 1: 46-55).

Two mothers with pure hearts, ready and available to God's Spirit and responsive to angelic visitations that pronounced to them how God wanted to use them for his glory. Because of their upright hearts, responsive and receptive to the movement of God's Spirit, the Lord saw fit to have them be the mothers of John the Baptist and his cousin the Lord Jesus. Mothers with strong maternal instincts, we know them both as pure vessels of God, living fully their privileged status as faithful servants of the King of kings and Lord of lords. Their hearts were kept pure by the Spirit who empowered them and by the Lord who lavished love upon them.

Purity of heart is a gift that only comes from the movement of God's Spirit, as he calls, convicts, purifies, equips, and empowers us as Christ followers into life in all its abundance. For Mary and Elizabeth, their pure hearts were blessed mightily by God (King David echoes this sentiment, "to the pure you show yourself pure" in 2 Samuel 22:27). But for most others, a purified heart is one that experiences the purifying process in the furnace of transformation, which ultimately leads the faithful to a distinct unity with God. Like King David after coming clean from his free-fall into lying, adultery and murder, he finally cries out to God, "Create in me a pure heart, O God" (Psalm 51: 10).

Keeping ourselves pure is not simply a human effort (which is a must!), but is most significantly a work of God's Spirit who leads us into and empowers us with self-control so that we can maintain purity of heart. No one can claim purity of heart for oneself, and the one who does is living in self-deceit. As children of God, we put our hope in the love of the Father, who calls us children of God, and therefore "everyone who has this hope in him purifies himself, just as he is pure" (1 John 3:3). Choosing to have our hearts purified by the Father, the Holy Spirit, and the Gospel of Christ, we make ourselves fully available to the Lord by offering our lives as living sacrifices, holy and pleasing to God (Romans 12: 1).

The worship song, "Purify My Heart" invites the Refiner's fire to purify the heart, letting it be as gold, pure gold…to be holy; set apart for the Lord; set apart for the Master, ready to do his will. But in order for that to occur, the heat of the fire is there to cleanse the believer from deep within the heart and soul. Cleansing, forgiving, restoring, and renewing the life of the faithful one is what God desires – and ultimately delivers to those who enter this life–changing process of sanctification. If this is the longing of your heart, then I invite you to pray, "Cleanse me with hyssop, and I will be clean; wash me, and I will be whiter than snow. Let me hear joy and gladness; let the bones you have crushed rejoice. Hide your face from my sins and blot out all my iniquity. Create in me a pure heart, O God, and renew a steadfast spirit within me. Do not cast me away from your presence or take your Holy Spirit from me. Restore to me the joy of your salvation and grant me a willing spirit, to sustain me" (Psalm 51: 7-12).

Day 26

Journal: Reflections on My Pure Heart

_____

_____

_____

_____

_____

_____

_____

_____

_____

_____

_____

_____

_____

_____

_____

_____

_____

_____

_____

Day 27

✏

The Bitter Heart

Broken. Hurt. Angry. Bitter. An emotional regression and a downward spiral toward division...all too often evidenced in the wider world, even in the church, and sadly even in the home. Bitterness is poison to the heart and the fruit of bitterness is destructive to all who lie in her pathway. Many who are bitter direct their rage toward God, blaming and casting responsibility purposefully or inadvertently in God's direction. Some blame others, deflecting their bitterness toward those who supposedly created the bitterness in their heart. No matter the source, the fruits growing out from the root of bitterness are many. One pastor describes them as "defilement, division, deadness, deception, depression, delirium, damage, and distraction." Not the kind of fruit any person of faith would want attached to their life!

And, as long as Satan can convince, confuse, and condemn you to believe your bitterness is justified, you will be enticed to remain in the prison of your bitter heart. Yes, the bitter heart is in jail, locked behind the bars of disillusionment and destruction. Job, who has many reasons to remain in such a locked up state of heart and mind, speaks openly of his bitterness: "I will not refrain my mouth; I will speak in the anguish of my spirit; I will complain in the bitterness of my soul (Job 7:11); "My soul is weary of my life; I will leave my complaint on myself; I will speak in the bitterness of my soul" (Job 10:1). But in the end, even Job is delivered from such emotional prison and "the Lord made him prosperous again and gave him twice as much as he had before; the Lord blessed the latter part of Job's life more than the first" (Job 42: 10, 12).

Choosing to stay in a state of bitterness is foolishness. For in a state of bitterness one is kept away from the landscape of joy. A bitter heart is thorny, prickly, and likened to a porcupine, keeping every living object at a distance or harshly struck by the piercing arrows of bitter hatred. To know one with a bitter heart is to see a life wither away into a sorely troubled, emaciated life without much beyond the skeleton of basic existence. Like seeing a starving child or sickly adult, the bitter hearted one is left to struggle simply to breathe and exist. Alone, desperate, troubled, and defiled, the bitter heart is headed to self destruction and spiritual death.

"Each heart knows its own bitterness, and no one else can share its joy" (Proverbs 14: 10). Bitterness is what one keeps in one's heart, no matter if it's ever shared by the company of others. I know too many bitter people who refuse to admit their brokenness, inner turmoil, emotional abuse, neglect, and collusion. Instead of seeking reconciliation and forgiveness, they hold fast to their angry deception and they are dying a slow, painful relational death, as are those who surround them. The Apostle Paul speaks directly to such bitter hearts, "Get rid of all bitterness, rage and anger, brawling and slander, along with every form of malice. Be kind and compassionate to one another, forgiving each other, just as in Christ God forgave you" (Ephesians 4: 31,32).

"See to it that no one misses the grace of God and that no bitter root grows up to cause trouble and defile many" (Hebrews 12: 15). For, "Anyone who claims to be in the light but hates his brother is still in the darkness" (1 John 2:9). "But if you harbor bitter envy and selfish ambition in your hearts, do not boast about it or deny the truth...for where you have envy and selfish ambition, there you find disorder and every evil practice, but the wisdom that comes from heaven is first of all pure; then peace loving, considerate, submissive, full of mercy and good fruit, impartial and sincere" (James 3: 14, 16, 17). These biblical truths speak directly to the one who harbors bitterness in the heart. One does not have to live in such a prison; the love of Jesus can indeed set one free to live a life of grace, mercy, peace, and joy.

Are you harboring bitterness in your heart today? To whom or what do you attribute your bitterness? Is it time to be set free from the bondage of your bitter heart? If so, then say yes to the invitation to freedom, grace, and joy in the Lord.

Confess your bitterness. Own your brokenness and the hurt you've caused and received from another. Release your anger and don't let it keep a hold on your heart any longer. Pray that God's Spirit will cast away the enemy's desire for self and relational destruction. Choose to walk in a renewed and transformed way of being. Don't turn back; let go and let God heal, strengthen, and restore. Instead of a bitter heart, trust God for a better heart. Allow the Father, Son and Holy Spirit to reign supreme in your heart...with God fully resident in your heart; there will no longer be room for bitterness.

Day 27

Journal: Reflections on My Bitter Heart

_____

_____

_____

_____

_____

_____

_____

_____

_____

_____

_____

_____

_____

_____

_____

_____

_____

_____

_____

_____

_____

Day 28

❦

The Trusting Heart

A trusting heart begins with saying yes to the invitation from the Lord to trust him with all your heart…"and lean not on your own understanding; in all your ways submit to him, and he will make your paths straight. Do not be wise in your own eyes; fear the Lord and shun evil. This will bring health to your body and nourishment to your bones. Honor the Lord with your wealth, with the first fruits of all your crops; then your barns will be filled to overflowing, and your vats will brim over with new wine" (Proverbs 3: 5-12). These proverbs are packed with wisdom, for trusting God allows us the joy of putting our life in his faithful hands so that we enjoy health and vitality in all aspects of our life, including our livelihood, avocations, and relationships.

Out of that relationship of trust in God, we become a trustworthy person. Jesus makes it clear that it's important to be known by others as reliable, dependable, and true to our word. "Whoever can be trusted with very little can also be trusted with much, and whoever is dishonest with very little will also be dishonest with much. So if you have not been trustworthy in handling worldly wealth, who will trust you with true riches? And if you have not been trustworthy with someone else's property, who will give you property of your own?" (Luke 16: 10-12). Living a life of integrity and trustworthiness is by far one of the best legacies any one could leave behind for future generations. May it be so for you and me as Christ followers today.

Those who trust in the Lord and have grown as a trustworthy friend, also take the risk in trusting others. When we know that all healthy relationships are based on the foundation of trust, we incline our hearts toward others hoping for trusting responses. "Love does not delight in evil but rejoices with the truth. It always protects, always trusts, always hopes, always perseveres" (1 Corinthians 13: 6,7). If trust is the bedrock of our relationship with God and others, then love is what holds us all together. Let love be your guide in reaching out to another and inviting them into your life. Listen intently to others, encourage one another, pursue health among others, and learn the secret of contentment in all of your earthly relationships. It's worth the risk!

Eventually, since we don't live in a bubble, trust between others will be breached. Our expectations may be shattered by a disappointment that ensues between spouses, friends, colleagues, and/or associates. A trusting heart desires more than anything to restore a broken trust. "Therefore, as God's chosen people, holy and dearly loved, clothe yourselves with compassion, kindness, humility, gentleness and patience. Bear with each other and forgive one another if any of you has a grievance against someone. Forgive as the Lord forgave you. And over all these virtues put on love, which binds them all together in perfect unity" (Colossians 3: 12-14). Reaching out with an earnest desire to restore a broken relationship is the evidence of a trusting heart. It takes concerted effort and prayer to bring about restitution, but it's worth the time it takes to do so.

However, there are times in life when it seems impossible to reconcile, and even for a time it might be best to release those you simply cannot trust. The Apostle Paul wrestled with that as he sought to reconcile who would be most responsive to the gospel. Would it be the Jew or the Gentile, the slave or the freeman? Would all come to a living faith in Jesus, or would there be rejection of the truth even among people of faith? "See, I lay in Zion a stone that causes people to stumble and a rock that makes them fall, and the one who believes in him will never be put to shame" (Romans 9:33). In real life today, it may not simply be those who reject the gospel, but within the faith community those who reject one another. This happens all too often, so we need to learn how to hold all relationships with open-handed trust and not force the necessary change(s) that lead to full reconciliation.

No matter what may come of our relationships with others, we can indeed depend fully on God and put our trust in the Lord. He cares deeply about all of the circumstances and relationships of our lives. He is there and he concerns himself with all the details of our complex lives. Jesus reminds his followers, "Do not let your hearts be troubled. You believe in God; believe also in me" (John 14:1). So may we take seriously our trust in the Lord all the days of our lives - in the good times, hard times, and everything in between. "May the God of hope fill you with all joy and peace as you trust in him, so that you may overflow with hope by the power of the Holy Spirit" (Romans 15:13). Will you continue to develop a trusting heart, no matter what may come your way today?

Day 28

Journal: Reflections on My Trusting Heart

_____

_____

_____

_____

_____

_____

_____

_____

_____

_____

_____

_____

_____

_____

_____

_____

_____

_____

_____

Day 29

The Fearful Heart

As a child I was fearful of the dark. Leaving a light on in the hallway and bathroom helped me feel safe. As an adolescent I developed a fear of fire. This most likely came from two house fires, which were devastating for families we loved. Living with fears can be debilitating, and people with fears and/or phobias are not to be ignored or ridiculed. No matter how fearful a heart can become, God understands and stands ready to heal. He's done so in many hearts and lives throughout the generations.

Having a fear-filled heart is different from the "fear of the Lord" that the Scriptures encourage. Developing a healthy fear of the Lord means that the believer is in worshipful awe at the magnificence and majesty of God, trusting wholeheartedly in the promises, protection, and peace of God. "The fear of the Lord is the beginning of wisdom," we read in the Psalms (Psalm 111) and Proverbs (Proverbs 9:10). To fear God in this regard is good for the soul. A healthy, reverential fear of God leads one to a deeper trust in and a greater conviction about the Lord: it's where wisdom begins.

Fears that aren't led toward awe and reverence are those that hinder a vital relationship with God. When we hold onto our fears, either willfully or inadvertently, the fear itself can become at minimum a distraction, and can possibly become an idol in our soul (growing larger and more all consuming than God). The fear can cripple us from moving forward. It can damage relationships and diminish one's effectiveness.

Fears come in multiple shapes and sizes. The list of phobias from A to Z numbers 100 or more. Some of the fears include the fears of flying, of crowds, of being touched, of thunder and lightening, of failure, of being alone, of clowns, of speaking in public, of needles/injections, and of strangers, just to name a few. To grip onto our fears and not let them go is to allow them to reign captive in our hearts. Hope is the antidote to fear, and hope is what needs to be proclaimed to those captivated by their fears. Disclosing one's phobia to trusted family and friends is the beginning of the healing process. God uses his people as his hands and voice of hope of renewal.

For the less than incapacitating fears (those that don't require psychological treatment or therapeutic attention), there is certainly hope for those who struggle with a fearful heart. To begin with, God isn't the source of our fearful heart. Instead, he longs to give every believer a spirit of power and love and self-control (2 Timothy 1:7). God's great gift to all members of his family is love, and since God is love, "There is no fear in love. But perfect love drives out fear, because fear has to do with punishment. The one who fears is not made perfect in love" (1 John 4: 18). This is followed by one of the most significant truths of all, "We love because he first loved us" (1 John 4:19). It's because of God's first love that our fears can be driven out of our hearts and replaced with loving and gentle peace.

Is there a fear in your heart that you'd like to have removed by God and replaced with his love...love that is filled with confidence and contentment? Invite those you trust into the story of your fearfulness. Ask them to give you the courage to pursue grace and healing. Embrace the freedom to confess your fear and entrust it into the gentle hands of God to redeem and transform it for his greater glory, first in your own heart and then in your daily witness to all who cross your path. May your fearful heart be radically transformed into a trusting heart today.

Day 29

Journal: Reflections on My Fearful Heart

_____

_____

_____

_____

_____

_____

_____

_____

_____

_____

_____

_____

_____

_____

_____

_____

_____

_____

_____

_____

_____

Day 30

∞

The Contrite Heart

The convicted, broken, contrite heart that's receptive to the will of God is a sweet offering sure to be blessed of God. To offer our brokenness to God by way of a contrite spirit is showing sincere remorse, regret and/or sorrow for our daily sins or offenses. Literally meaning, "worn out, ground to pieces" the word contrite is ideally suited for the image of a heart broken open for a deeper work of forgiveness and sanctification to occur.

For those who are more pliable to the Spirit, a contrite attitude toward our brokenness and our desperate need for God is trustingly displayed. You may have heard about the sculptor who after finishing his work of art sees that there's a crack in it. Knowing that it was imperfect, he decides to start over. He breaks the sculpture into pieces and then adds water. Once he does so, the sculpture became clay once more and he is able to re-create his work of art. So it is with our lives, imperfect and flawed, needing to be broken and forgiven, we become whole once more by the gentle and loving hand of God the Master Artist.

For many, however, the genuine nature of a contrite heart meets internal resistance due to our pride and stubbornness. A contrite heart requires mourning over and regretting remorsefully our sinfulness and disobedience to God's commands. The essence of the gospel is that once admitting our arrogance and pride and submitting our lives into the hands of the Sculpture God, we are baptized as the water of his grace softens the hardened clay of our brittle hearts. When we encounter defiance in our heart toward the need to become malleable to God, a spiritual wall is erected between God and our soul.

King David had a hard time coming to recognize his need for a broken, contrite heart after his sin of adultery with Bathsheba, his sin of murder toward Uriah her husband, and his sin of lying to God and others about his multiple offenses (read 2 Samuel 11 for the detailed story). It wasn't until he was confronted by Nathan the prophet (2 Samuel 12), that he finally was convicted of his sinfulness, and was broken and contrite before the Lord. Here was the shepherd boy turned king, leading the people of God, his army and officers, a musician and psalmist unlike any other, suffering from the struggle of running away from the most important response of all: repentance.

Psalm 51 is considered his tome on confession, forgiveness, and faithfulness – all ensuing as a result of his broken, contrite heart. It's the way we too must think and feel about our own sin, and our desperate need for God's merciful touch of healing. He owns his sin and turns to God, "Have mercy on me, O God, according to your unfailing love; according to your compassion blot out my transgressions" (vs. 1). He prays for cleansing, "Cleanse me with hyssop, and I will be clean" (vs. 7). He pleads for renewal, "Create in me a pure heart, O God, and renew a steadfast spirit within me" (vs. 10). He delights in his restoration,

"Restore to me the joy of your salvation and grant me a willing spirit to sustain me" (vs. 12).

Psalm 51 proclaims the goodness of God and the righteousness of the people of God, "The sacrifices of God are a broken spirit; a broken and contrite heart, O God, you will not despise" (vs. 17). Yes, a contrite heart is what pleases and honors God and brings about his favor (cf. Isaiah 61). This is foundational to everything in life. Being a Christian means being broken and contrite – for this is the flavor of deep unending joy, peace, praise, and witness. Jonathan Edwards said it well, "All gracious affections that are a sweet aroma to Christ are brokenhearted affections. A truly Christian love, either to God or men, is a humble brokenhearted love" (Religious Affections, p. 339). Will you open up yourself to God with a contrite heart today?

Journal: Reflections on My Contrite Heart

_____

_____

_____

_____

_____

_____

_____

_____

_____

_____

_____

_____

_____

_____

_____

_____

_____

_____

_____

_____

_____

Day 31

Day 31

The Loving Heart

To speak of God, his Word, and the life he invites us to fulfill would be incomplete without the sheer mention of the word love. Love is the heart of the gospel, and a loving heart is what the Lord wants of us more than anything else. His love toward us is almost indescribable and yet the Scriptures remind us that it's unfailing, unconditional, and everlasting. It's wrapped up in the personhood of God, Father, Son and Holy Spirit. And, his love is made manifest in his creation, among his people, and through his life-changing transformation from darkness into light.

The most declarative statement of God's desire for us to have a loving heart is found in the Great Commandments: to love God with heart, soul, mind and strength, and to love our neighbors as we love ourselves (Deuteronomy 6; Matthew 22). Upon these two commandments hang all other imperatives to love and serve in Jesus' name. To miss this focus is to miss the very heart of God. And, to ignore this directive is to walk in disobedience. "Listen!" says the Lord, to the Beloved Son, Jesus, recalled both at his baptism and at the transfiguration (Matthew 3 and 17). The message of Jesus is summarized in one word: love. That's the message we are to receive in our hearts and offer generously to others in Jesus' name.

On the Mount of Beatitudes, we listen in on one of the most loving sermons to come from the voice of Jesus. It's here where Jesus outlines the ways in which he longs for his disciples to live a life of love and to express a heart of love. In his Sermon on the Mount Jesus gives a picture of the heart of the true people of God, those who are a part of his Kingdom and have the full blessings of the Kingdom. A heart full of love embodies these attributes:

"Blessed are the poor in spirit, for theirs is the kingdom of heaven.Blessed are those who mourn, for they will be comforted. Blessed are the meek, for they will inherit the earth. Blessed are those who hunger and thirst for righteousness, for they will be filled. Blessed are the merciful, for they will be shown mercy. Blessed are the pure in heart, for they will see God. Blessed are the peacemakers, for they will be called children of God. Blessed are those who are persecuted because of righteousness, for theirs is the kingdom of heaven. Blessed are you when people insult you, persecute you and falsely say all kinds of evil against you because of me. Rejoice and be glad, because great is your reward in heaven" (Matt. 5: 3-12).

Elsewhere Jesus invites his followers to remain in his love and fulfill the mandate: "Love each other as I have loved you. Greater love has no one than this, that he lay down his life for his friends" (John 15: 9-13). Jesus demonstrated this kind of love first and foremost to his closest disciples, but also to those who daily crossed his path. The Apostle Paul reiterates these truths by stating with clarity what a loving heart looks like: it is patient, kind, rejoices with the truth, always trusts, hopes and perseveres. It's not envious, boastful, proud, rude, self-seeking, easily angered, nor does it delight in evil (1 Cor. 13: 5-8).

None of these passages require much commentary. All are very self-explanatory. Meditate on these few passages and a heart full of love will be revealed and offered to you today. One either has a heart of love based upon and motivated by the love of God, or one has a heart that's directed selfishly toward interests contrary to God. What is your choice today? Will you receive the love of God into your heart and invite His Spirit to create within you a loving heart toward others? May it be so!

Day 31

Journal: Reflections on My Loving Heart

_____

_____

_____

_____

_____

_____

_____

_____

_____

_____

_____

_____

_____

_____

_____

_____

_____

_____

_____

_____

About the Author

Stephen A. Macchia is the founding president of Leadership Transformations, Inc. (LTI), a ministry focusing on the spiritual formation needs of leaders and the spiritual discernment processes of leadership teams in local church and parachurch ministry settings. In conjunction with his leadership of LTI, he also serves as the director of the Pierce Center for Disciple-Building at Gordon-Conwell Theological Seminary. He is the author of several books, including *Becoming a Healthy Church, Becoming a Healthy Disciple, Becoming A Healthy Team,* and *Crafting A Rule of Life*. Stephen and his wife, Ruth, are the proud parents of Nathan and Rebekah and reside in Lexington, Massachusetts.

For more information about Stephen A. Macchia or Leadership Transformations, Inc., visit:

www.LeadershipTransformations.org
www.HealthyChurch.net
www.RuleOfLife.com

Other Titles by Stephen A. Macchia

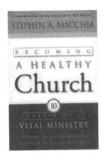

In **Becoming a Healthy Church**, Stephen A. Macchia illustrates how to move beyond church growth to church health. Healthy growth is a process that requires risk taking, lifestyle changes, and ongoing evaluation. This book is a practical, hands-on manual to launch you and your church into a process of positive change. Available in 3 Languages: English, Spanish, Korean.

Becoming a Healthy Disciple explores the ten traits of a healthy disciple, including a vital prayer life, evangelistic outreach, worship, servanthood, and stewardship. He applies to individual Christians the ten characteristics of a healthy church outlined in his previous book, Becoming a Healthy Church. Discipleship is a lifelong apprenticeship to Jesus Christ, the master teacher. Macchia looks to John the beloved disciple as an example of a life lived close to Christ.

Becoming a Healthy Disciple Small Group Study & Worship Guide is a companion to Steve Macchia's book, *Becoming a Healthy Disciple*. This small group guide provides discussion and worship outlines to enrich your study of the ten traits of a healthy disciple. This 12-week small group resource provides Study, Worship, and Prayer guidelines for each session.

Becoming a Healthy Team is essential for building the kingdom. Stephen A. Macchia offers tried and tested principles and practices to help your leadership team do the same. He'll show you how to Trust, Empower, Assimilate, Manage, and Serve. That spells TEAMS and ultimately success. Filled with scriptural guideposts, Becoming a Healthy Team provides practical answers and pointed questions to keep your team on track and moving ahead.

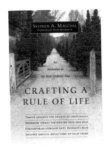

In **Crafting a Rule of Life** Stephen A. Macchia looks to St. Benedict as a guide for discovering your own rule of life in community. It is a process that takes time and concerted effort; you must listen to God and discern what he wants you to be and do for his glory. But through the basic disciplines of Scripture, prayer and reflection in a small group context this practical workbook will lead you forward in a journey toward Christlikeness.

Additional Resouces @
SPIRITUALFORMATIONSTORE.COM

Guide to Prayer for All Who Walk With God

The latest from Rueben Job, A Guide to Prayer for All Who Walk With God offers a simple pattern of daily prayer built around weekly themes and organized by the Christian church year. Each week features readings for reflection from such well-known spiritual writers as Francis of Assisi, Teresa of Avila, Dietrich Bonhoeffer, Henri J. M. Nouwen, Sue Monk Kidd, Martin Luther, Julian of Norwich, M. Basil Pennington, Evelyn Underhill, Douglas Steere, and many others.

Guide to Prayer for All Who Seek God

For nearly 20 years, people have turned to the Guide to Prayer series for a daily rhythm of devotion and personal worship. Thousands of readers appreciate the series' simple structure of daily worship, rich spiritual writings, lectionary guidelines, and poignant prayers. Like its predecessors, A Guide to Prayer for All Who Seek God will become a treasured favorite for those hungering for God as the Christian year unfolds.

Guide to Prayer for Ministers and Other Servants

A best-seller for more than a decade! This classic devotional and prayer book includes thematically arranged material for each week of the year as well as themes and schedules for 12 personal retreats. The authors have adopted the following daily format for this prayer book: daily invocations, readings, scripture, reflection, prayers, weekly hymns, benedictions, and printed psalms.

Guide to Prayer for All God's People

A compilation of scripture, prayers and spiritual readings, this inexhaustible resource contains thematically arranged material for each week of the year and for monthly personal retreats. Its contents have made it a sought-after desk reference, a valuable library resource and a cherished companion.

LEADERSHIP
TRANSFORMATIONS INC.
FORMATION | DISCERNMENT | RENEWAL

- Soul Care Retreats and Soul Sabbaths
- Emmaus: Spiritual Leadership Communities
- Selah: Spiritual Direction Certificate Program
- Spiritual Formation Groups
- Spiritual Health Assessments
- Spiritual Discernment for Teams
- Sabbatical Planning
- Spiritual Formation Resources

Visit www.LeadershipTransformations.org

or call (877) TEAM LTI.

Made in the USA
Middletown, DE
17 April 2015